Signatures

Enslaved

A Chronicle of Resistance

Book 4 - A Companion Reader

By
Brian Sankarsingh

SG Productions

First Edition 2023

All rights reserved.

No part of this publication may be reproduced in any form, or by any means, electronic or mechanical, including photocopying, recording, or any information browsing, storage, or retrieval system without permission in writing from SG Productions except in the case of brief quotations embodied in critical reviews and certain other non-commercial uses permitted by copyright law.

For permission requests, write to:
Sankarsingh Gonsalves Productions
c\o brian@sgproductions.ca

ISBN
Softcover - 978-1-7380419-4-7
Hardcover - 978-1-7380419-5-4

History

Praise for Enslaved, A Chronicle of Resistance

"Enslaved" is a very worthy book series! Especially for educational institutions. I am indeed happy to endorse and promote "the Enslaved series" at A Different Booklist bookstore! – **Itah Sadu, award-winning storyteller and author, managing director of the Blackhurst Cultural Centre and co-owner of A Different Booklist.**

Overall, the book (Enslaved, A Chronicle of Resistance Lamentation of the Enslaved) with a focus on the beginning period of enslavement is a very good educational tool or resource mainly for young adults and youth. It introduces them to the facts of the Atlantic Slave Trade. Young people might not necessarily want to read a textbook account about African enslavement. Poetry can be more digestible at times, and it is an alternative way to expose them to that history and to important related themes. For example, that there was much resistance on the part of the enslaved; and they did not just passively accept the brutality imposed on them. I also appreciated the poems: "Stripped" and "I am Human" because they made very clear that the only way for the enslavement of Africans to happen on such a monstrous scale was by the belief that Africans were not fully human. It is an important point to make because it introduced a conversation about the immorality of the entire practice. People need to know not only the facts and details of what happened, but why it happened and also why it should never happen again." **Geeta Raghunanan, A Different Booklist**

***

First and foremost, I feel privileged to have been asked to review this amazing work by a good friend and colleague. I don't consider myself a literary person nor I consider myself a person engaged with history as such. I like to read, and I attempt to familiarize myself with history with the aim of understanding the present.

I am honored to lead an organization established to address the impact of anti-Black racism on the health and wellbeing of Black communities. Reading the series 'Enslaved, A Chronicle of Resistance', not only re-affirmed for me the importance of the movement that uplifts the voice, the struggle, the strength and the dreams and aspirations of the diverse Black communities which was intensified after the painful deaths of George Floyd, Brianna Taylor, Regis Korchinski-Paquet, Joyce Echaquan and many more; but also reminded me that addressing systemic anti-Black racism is a very long and complex journey because it is hidden in plain sight!

Not all good will gestures by the system players are meant to bring about positive change and wellbeing for Black communities. In one of the poems, John Brown, the captain of the ship, has kept the vessel well ventilated. Plainly this is a noble gesture to keep his 'cargo' healthy. But hidden is the motive of preserving the value of the 'cargo' so there is no financial loss. How are we to receive certain legislations, policies, promises from the ship owners and captains of today? Do they have our true wellbeing in mind or does it continue to be about their own self-preservation? A question that continued to resonate with me as I navigated through the pages of the three volumes. "There is a moral to this story hidden in plain sight – not everyone who is fighting for you, may believe in your human right".

When you read about the establishment of the 'Apprenticeship Laws', you cannot but think about the current state of our child welfare system – "So come and give me your children I will make them apprentice, For you cannot even care for them and that fact hurts my conscience". You read about the 15th Amendment and the provision of voting rights. But you also learn about the introduction of the poll tax that prohibited many Black people from not only voting and having their voices heard but also denied them hope and choice.

Enslaved – A Chronicle of Resistance comprises of three volumes – The Lamentation of the Enslaved (set between 1700-1800), Freedom Bells are Ringing (1800-1900) and Hidden in Plain sight (present day). The volumes are connected by a very powerful refrain from the Kingdom of Nri (Nigeria), a kingdom of freedom and haven for marginalized peoples. "I am child of the Kingdom of Nri, We believe ALL men are born to be FREE. This gift is granted by Chukwu to all, That enter into Nri's great hall". We are all born FREE. And plainly we are all free where we live today. However, hidden in plain sight are many shackles, chains, constraints, limitations, barriers, and abuses.

Brain Sankarsingh brings these hidden and ongoing issues to the forefront through amazing poetic literature introduced by thought provoking and context setting introductions. One cannot but enjoy his work. – **Liben Gebremikael, Executive Director TAIBU Community Health Centre**

Table of contents

FOREWORD I
DEDICATIONS III
ACKNOWLEDGEMENTS.. IV
ABOUT CAPITALIZATIONS AND LANGUAGE CONVENTIONS............... V
INTRODUCTION VI

INDIGENOUS SLAVERY 1

THE ORIGINS OF INDIGENOUS SLAVERY 2
INDIGENOUS SLAVERY PRACTICES.. 5
CULTURAL IMPACT OF INDIGENOUS SLAVERY.................................. 8
DECLINE OF INDIGENOUS SLAVERY 12
LEGACY OF INDIGENOUS SLAVERY 16

THE ATLANTIC SLAVE TRADE 20

EUROPEAN EXPANSION 21
THE MIDDLE PASSAGE 25
UNEARTHING THE MYSTERIES OF THE KINGDOM OF NRI 29
THE TRIANGULAR TRADE 33
AFRICAN KINGDOMS AND THE SLAVE TRADE 37
IMPACT OF THE ATLANTIC SLAVE TRADE 41

AMERICAN SLAVERY 46

SLAVERY IN COLONIAL AMERICA 47
PLANTATION ECONOMY 50
SLAVE RESISTANCE AND REVOLTS.. 54
CULTURE AND IDENTITY 58
ABOLITIONIST MOVEMENTS AND THE ROAD TO FREEDOM 62

THE LEGACY OF AMERICAN SLAVERY 68

JIM CROW ERA AND SEGREGATION 69
CIVIL RIGHTS MOVEMENT 73
SYSTEMIC RACISM AND STRUCTURAL INEQUALITY 78
REPARATIONS AND RESTORATIVE JUSTICE 85
TOWARDS A MORE JUST FUTURE... 88

RESISTANCE AND ABOLITION 92

- Revolts and Uprisings 93
- Abolitionist Movements 96
- Underground Railroad and Freedom Networks 101
- International Abolition and Diplomacy 105
- Legacy of Resistance and Abolition 109

SLAVERY SYSTEMS 113

- Ancient Slavery in Greece and Rome 114
- Slavery in the Islamic World 119
- Slavery in the Caribbean and Latin America 123
- Slavery in Asia 127
- Slavery Systems – Amerindian and African 130

HISTORICAL PERSPECTIVES 133

- Eurocentric Vs. Afrocentric Perspectives 134
- Revisionist Interpretations 138
- Gender and Slavery 141
- Memory and Commemoration 144
- Teaching and Learning About Slavery 147

LESSONS FROM HISTORY 151

- Addressing Systemic Racism 152
- Social Justice Movements 156
- Healing and Reconciliation 160
- Promoting Equality and Inclusion 164

A FINAL THOUGHT 168

ABOUT THE AUTHOR 172

Foreword

I reiterate, at the outset, that I am extremely impressed with the general work and the power that flows off the page. It brings to mind – by virtue of its stridency, courage, and creativity – some of the writings of authors like James Baldwin, Maya Angelou, Lorraine Hansberry, George Jackson (whose 'Prison Letters' I was privileged to read, in my very early teens, very many moons ago).

The inclusion of historical fact, with division into three distinct eras, is ingenious. It accurately mirrors the seminal research done by the Caribbean's foremost economist and developmentalist, the late Lloyd Best and Canadian thinker Kari Levitt viz., the Plantation Economy (Pure Plantation, Plantation Modified & Plantation Further Modified – the latter corresponding to the current era). ENSLAVED focusses precisely on these eras, through a more personalized, dramatic, poetic lens.

The accurate portrayal of pre-slavery Africa and its economic and socio-political structures is another case in point. Detailing the horrors of the Slave Trade and the singularity of its profit maximization motive also enhances the work's historical accuracy. As does treatment of 'the white man's burden" – civilizing savages.

The roles of religion and systemic (institutional) racism in facilitating system perpetration and perpetuation, are also well recognized and presented. Well done!

There is a lot more that can be said about Enslaved, A Chronicle of Resistance, all of it complimentary. It would be great to see it added to the existing corpus of relevant literature, and it certainly has my best wishes.

James Baisden *(12-04-1957 - 15-03-2023)*
Educator, Author, Music Producer and Artist

Dedications

I am not a Black person, nor do I identify as a Black person. I am, however, a Person of Colour, and I do identify with the struggle of BIPOC peoples.

This book, therefore, is dedicated to Black people, Indigenous people, and People of Colour everywhere and to their continued resistance of White supremacy – **Brian Sankarsingh**

Acknowledgements

Without the support and perseverance of my beloved wife and life partner this book would not be possible. It is her strength and optimism that has fueled my own passion for this writing. She is my muse; encouraging, supporting, and inspiring me to pursue this crazy dream.

Researching and writing this book involved was so emotionally draining I am thankful for my friends Hari, Zee, and Kris - thank you for being there and giving me your support when it was sorely needed brothers.

The idea for Enslaved, A Chronicle of Resistance was conceived in the Summer of 2020 as I prepared to launch my first book. It began as a seed, and I realised that it would be a severe injustice to tend to it on my own. So started the search for other gardeners. There were several failed attempts and with each so grew my desperation. Then suddenly, in the space of a few weeks this talented group of poets came together.

About Capitalizations and Language Conventions

In this book, Enslaved, A Chronicle of Resistance, the poets have agreed to capitalize Black and White when referring to racial groups [i]. In the current climate of hate, demonization, and polarization we feel it is better to build bridges. This does not mean we diminish or ignore history, after all it is the path that brought us to this place. We risk much more than division between races if we choose to ignore history, we risk our humanity.

We use Canada English conventions in the book.

Introduction

The idea for adding a fourth book to the series, came whilst looking over the research I had done to write - and lead the writing of - the series itself. This companion reader affords you the opportunity to understand the actual historical context of the poetry. It tracks what is going on in the wider world and then brings it back to the books themselves. This book therefore, is a true companion to:

1. Enslaved A Chronicle of Resistance Book I – The Lamentation of the Enslaved
2. Enslaved A Chronicle of Resistance Book II – Freedom Bells are Ringing
3. Enslaved A Chronicle of Resistance Book III – Hidden in Plain Sight

Poems from these books are referenced throughout this one in the following manner.

Reference Poems
<<Book Name>>
- <<Poem Name>>

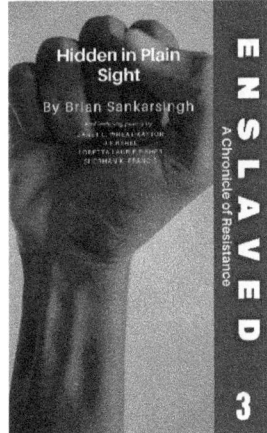
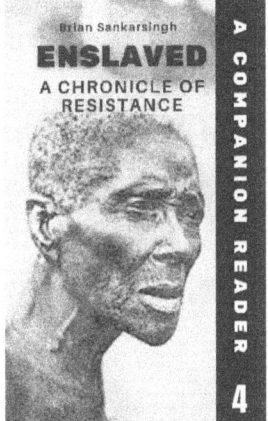

In the grand tapestry of human existence, there are threads that intertwine and create patterns that shape the course of nations. One such thread, a thread born of exploitation and oppression, tightened its way across continents and across time, leaving a haunting legacy of torture and injustice. But where did this thread begin? Where did it take root, growing into the wicked tree of slavery that cast its ominous shadow over humanity? The journey starts with the loss of the Amerindian slaves, a loss that set the stage for the Atlantic slave trade.

As a writer, poet and person of colour, I set about seeking to uncover the truth of enslavement. I wanted to help those forgotten voices tell their story of enslavement. To give them the opportunity to tell the story of their pain and despair but also of their resilience and hope. It is a tale that needs to be told and heard, for only by understanding our past can we truly shape our future.

The story begins in the lands now known as the Americas, where the indigenous people, the Amerindians, led vibrant and flourishing civilizations. These proud nations thrived on the fertile soil and reveled in the abundance of nature around them. But as the winds of change swept through the continent, their world was irrevocably altered.

When the arrival of European explorers, like Christopher Columbus, brought disease and violence, the Amerindians faced a merciless enemy. Their population dwindled, and their once mighty empires collapsed under the weight of despair. The bond they had with the land, the connection that made them one with nature, was severed, leaving them vulnerable and desperate.

It was in this desperate state that the Amerindians became the first victims of a growing appetite for free labour. Europeans, eager to exploit the wealth of the newly discovered lands, saw the Amerindians as that source of free labour. The enslaved were the backbone of colonization, toiling under the scorching sun and facing unimaginable hardships. But as the Amerindian population continued to decline, a new solution had to be found to feed the insatiable hunger for labour.

And so, the focus shifted to the shores of Africa, where a new chapter in the shady saga of slavery would be written. The Atlantic slave trade, a harrowing episode in human history, was born. The lure of profit blinded the European powers to the humanity of their actions, and millions of Africans were torn from their homes, their families, and their land. They were forced into ships that sailed across the treacherous waters, their bodies stacked like so much cargo, as if they were not human but mere possessions.

The journey to the Americas was a cruel and degrading one. Many would not survive the ill-treatment, starvation, and disease. Those who did arrive were subjected to an existence of backbreaking labour, enduring the whip and the chains that bound them. But it was the thing that set the Africans apart that also made them ideal slaves. Their natural immunity to European diseases and their physical strength became their downfall. The Atlantic slave trade became the lifeblood of the American colonies, fueling their economic growth but staining their souls with the blood and tears of those enslaved.

But how did this evolving system of exploitation develop into the American slavery that we know today? How did the loss of the Amerindian slaves pave the way for the entrenchment of African slavery on American soil? These are the questions that we will explore together, seeking to unearth the hidden truths and shine a light on the interconnectedness of historical events.

So, dear reader, I invite you to join me on this journey through time. Let us venture into the depths of human suffering and triumph, unraveling the mysteries of our collective past. It is a tale that will both shock and inspire, for through understanding we can strive for a better future. Together, let us turn the page and peel back the layers of history to reveal the horrifying truth hidden beneath the surface.

Brian Sankarsingh

Indigenous Slavery

The Origins of Indigenous Slavery

The beginnings and deep roots of indigenous slavery can be found in the practice in warfare. In many indigenous societies, conflicts and territorial disputes were a common occurrence. It is no surprise, then, that prisoners of war were often subjected to enslavement. Captives were seen as spoils of battle, mere commodities to be bought, sold, and traded. The harsh reality was that surviving wars often meant being forced into a life of terrible servitude.

Reference Poems
The Lamentation of the Enslaved – Book 1
- A History Lesson – The Beginning

But warfare alone does not account for the origins of indigenous slavery. A deeper understanding is to be found by exploring the social hierarchy within these societies. In many indigenous cultures, social status and wealth were closely intertwined. Slavery often emerged as a direct result of social inequalities, with members of what were culturally accepted, lower classes being reduced to a life of servitude. This practice was often codified through various systems of law and understood as a natural consequence of one's social birthright. Those born into poverty or lower classes had little hope of escaping their predetermined fate.

As with any system of oppression, economic factors played a significant role in the propagation of indigenous slavery. In indigenous societies that relied heavily on agriculture or resource extraction, the demand for labour was high. Slavery, therefore, became an integral part of economic practices, allowing for the exploitation of enslaved individuals for the benefit of the ruling class. The labour of these slaves, often used in fields or mines, ensured the continued prosperity of the privileged few.

It is important to remember that the origins of indigenous slavery were not isolated to a single region or culture. Slavery was an unfortunate reality across the Americas, existing in various forms among the Aztecs, Mayans, Incans, and many other indigenous societies. The specific circumstances and practices of indigenous slavery varied, but the underlying power dynamics remained constant.

The enslavement of indigenous peoples by indigenous peoples did not go unnoticed by European colonizers. In fact, it was this already existing system of indigenous slavery that provided a framework for the transatlantic slave trade. Europeans, seeking to exploit the vast resources of the Americas, found it convenient to exploit the labour of indigenous slaves. However, as the demand for labour grew and the indigenous population dwindled due to disease and warfare, European colonizers turned their gaze to the African continent, thus opening a horrific chapter in human history.

It is crucial that we recognize the origins of indigenous slavery as not something inherent to the indigenous peoples themselves, but rather a result of larger societal structures and power imbalances. It is not enough to simply condemn the atrocities of the transatlantic slave trade without acknowledging the historical context from which it emerged. The origins of indigenous slavery lie in a complex web of warfare, social hierarchy, and economic practices. They serve as a stark reminder of the dark chapters in our shared history and humanity's enduring legacy of injustice. By examining the origins of indigenous slavery, we can better understand the depths of human suffering and the urgent need for justice and healing in our contemporary world. However, we must be able to balance our understanding of the horrors and injustice of slavery with what we see happening in our present day. The racism and polarization that we see rearing its head once again did not occur overnight. It carries with it enormous amounts of history passed on from generation to generation.

Indigenous Slavery Practices

When we examine the historical timeline, we realize that the methods of capturing, trading, and using indigenous slaves within their respective societies were present for a very long time. Indigenous slavery practices can be traced back to the earliest civilizations in the Americas, long before the arrival of European colonizers.

In the pre-Columbian era, many indigenous tribes engaged in warfare as a means of acquiring land, resources, and power. Slavery was an integral part of these conflicts, with captured individuals often becoming slaves to the victorious tribe. The methods used to capture these slaves varied depending on the tribe and the region, but they often involved ambushes, raids, and surprise attacks on enemy settlements.

Once captured, the fate of these indigenous slaves was highly dependent on their roles within their respective societies. Some were used as manual labourers, working in fields, mines, and construction projects. Others served as domestic servants, attending to the needs of their masters and their families. Regardless of their specific tasks, slaves had no legal rights or protections. They could be bought, sold, and inherited just like any other form of property.

The treatment of indigenous slaves within their societies also varied, depending on factors such as the wealth and social status of their owners. Those owned by powerful chiefs or nobles might receive relatively favorable treatment, with access to better living conditions and privileges. However, most indigenous slaves were subject to harsh living and working conditions, often enduring physical abuse, neglect, and emotional suffering.

The implications of indigenous enslavement were far-reaching and profound. For one, it perpetuated a cycle of violence and warfare that ravaged indigenous communities. The constant threat of capture and enslavement created a climate of fear and mistrust, pitting tribes against each other and leading to the destruction of many once-thriving societies.

Moreover, the introduction of European colonizers amplified the already existing indigenous slave trade. The arrival of the Spanish conquistadors in the 16th century paved the way for a wave of violence and exploitation, as the colonizers sought to extract vast amounts of wealth from the lands they claimed. Indigenous slaves were used extensively in this endeavor, forced to work in mines, plantations, and other labour-intensive industries.

The impacts of indigenous slavery were not limited to the Americas alone. The transatlantic slave trade, which brought millions of Africans to the Americas as slaves, was intimately connected to the indigenous slave trade. The skills and knowledge gained through centuries of enslaving indigenous populations were crucial in establishing the infrastructure and systems that facilitated the African slave trade.

Undoubtedly, the examination of indigenous slavery practices is a necessary component in understanding the full scope of the slave trade from Amerindian to African. It is a chapter in history that must be acknowledged and confronted, for it sheds light on the depths of human cruelty and the lasting legacy of oppression. When we take the time to look into the various methods of capturing, trading, and using indigenous slaves, as well as the roles they played, their treatment, and the implications of their enslavement, we can gain a more comprehensive understanding of this dark period in history and hopefully work towards a future where such atrocities are never repeated.

Cultural Impact of Indigenous Slavery

The social structures of indigenous societies underwent a profound transformation due to the introduction of slavery. As noted before, prior to the arrival of the Europeans, many indigenous societies practiced slavery within their own communities. However, this form of slavery was different from the later transatlantic slave trade. It was often predicated on capturing prisoners of war or those who committed crimes within the community. Still, it must be acknowledged that the enslavement of one's own people was not without its own cultural implications and ethical dilemmas.

With the arrival of the Europeans in the Americas, the dynamics of indigenous slavery underwent a radical change. The demands of the European colonizers for labour and resources pushed indigenous slavery beyond its previous boundaries. Tribes that had once engaged in localized forms of slavery suddenly found themselves thrust into a global system of human commerce and exploitation. This had a profound impact on their social structures, beliefs, and intertribal relationships.

One of the most immediate effects of the expansion of indigenous slavery was the disruption of traditional social structures. The capture and enslavement of individuals often led to the breakdown of families and kinship networks within indigenous communities. The forced separation of loved ones left a lasting scar on the collective memory of these societies. The loss and fragmentation of families tore at the very fabric of their social cohesion, leading to a sense of profound dislocation and generational trauma.

Additionally, the demand for labour from European colonizers disrupted the traditional division of labour within indigenous societies. Men, who were often the primary targets of European enslavement, were forcibly removed from their communities and subjected to grueling labour under harsh conditions. This created a significant gender imbalance within indigenous societies, as women were left to shoulder the burdens of both their traditional responsibilities and the added pressures of forced labour.

The introduction of indigenous slavery to the global market also had far-reaching consequences for the beliefs and spiritual practices of the tribes involved. The very foundations of indigenous ideologies were challenged by the dehumanizing nature of slavery. The concept of human beings as property, as commodities to be bought and sold, ran counter to their deeply ingrained beliefs in the sacredness of their own lives and the interconnectedness of all beings.

Moreover, the enslavement of indigenous peoples by Europeans often forced them to question the efficacy of their own spiritual practices. The Europeans, with their advanced technology and military might, were seen by many indigenous tribes as representatives of superior spiritual forces. The defeat and subjugation of native peoples by these seemingly invincible foreigners left many questioning the validity of their own belief systems. Some even adopted elements of the colonizers' religions in an attempt to salvage what remained of their once-powerful spiritual traditions.

The intertribal relationships within indigenous societies were also deeply impacted by the expansion of indigenous slavery. The capture and sale of individuals to European traders often resulted in strained relations between tribes. Some tribes actively participated in the slave trade, capturing members of neighboring tribes and selling them to Europeans for profit. This led to a breakdown of trust and cooperation among once-allied tribes, as the lure of wealth and power disrupted the delicate balance of tribal alliances.

The cultural and societal impact of indigenous slavery cannot be overstated. Its effects reverberated through the generations, leaving a lasting imprint on the collective memory of indigenous communities. The disruption of social structures, the erosion of traditional beliefs, and the strain on intertribal relationships were profound and irrevocable. Despite all of this, we must admire the resilience and strength of indigenous peoples. They survived this exploitation and oppression and were still able to preserve their cultural heritage and thrive against all odds.

Decline of Indigenous Slavery

The early history of the Americas reveals indigenous populations engaging in various forms of slavery, influenced by cultural, religious, economic, and social factors unique to each region. Slavery in pre-Columbian America was diverse, with some societies practicing labour exploitation while others utilized captives as sacrificial rituals. Despite the variations, slavery was an integral part of many indigenous societies.

With the arrival of European colonizers, however, things swiftly changed. The colonization process entailed the establishment of settler colonies, primarily led by European powers such as Spain, Portugal, Britain, and France. These colonizers sought to exploit the vast resources of the Americas, including its indigenous populations. Thus, European colonization became one of the main catalysts for the decline of indigenous slavery.

The Europeans, driven by their own ambitions, sought to establish a labour force to extract the newfound wealth of the Americas. The Native American population, with its advanced agricultural techniques and labour skills, appeared to be an ideal solution. The Europeans manipulated existing cultural practices and power dynamics to reinforce their control over these populations. Through coercion, violence, sowing division and the introduction of new economic systems, the Europeans were able to undermine indigenous slavery in favor of their own forms of forced labour.

Yet, it is important to remember that European colonization was not the sole factor responsible for the decline of indigenous slavery. The arrival of Europeans also brought with it a range of diseases that the indigenous populations had little immunity against. Deadly diseases such as smallpox, measles, and influenza spread rapidly among the indigenous communities, decimating their populations. The large-scale loss of life and the subsequent disruption to indigenous social structures greatly weakened their ability to sustain slavery within their societies.

As the native populations dwindled, so did their influence and power. The once thriving empires and chiefdoms gradually collapsed, and indigenous societies faced an internal struggle to redefine their identities in the face of European dominance. The changes within indigenous societies themselves, catalyzed by colonization and the devastation of diseases, further contributed to the decline of indigenous slavery.

The consequences of this decline were far-reaching, impacting both indigenous populations and the broader dynamics of slave trade in the Americas. For the indigenous peoples, the decline of their traditional systems of slavery had both positive and negative implications. On one hand, they were relieved from the oppressive yoke of forced labour imposed by their own kind. On the other, they were thrust into a tumultuous world dominated by a foreign power, where they faced new forms of exploitation and manipulation.

Eventually without the labour force provided by indigenous slavery, the European colonizers turned to other sources to sustain the burgeoning economic machinery of the New World. This led to the increased importation of African slaves to replace the, now diminishing, indigenous labour supply. Thus, the decline of indigenous slavery inadvertently fueled the expansion of the transatlantic slave trade, with devastating consequences for African societies and the African diaspora.

In the wake of the decline of indigenous slavery, a complicated web of power dynamics and cultural assimilation began to shape the Americas. Indigenous populations, stripped of their autonomy and subjected to European rule, faced the erasure of their heritage, and were subjected to numerous forms of discrimination and marginalization. Their customs, traditions, and languages were suppressed, and they were forced to adapt to European cultural norms, further exacerbating their vulnerability to exploitation.

The waning of indigenous slavery also marked a significant shift in the global perception of slavery. As Europeans began to pursue African slaves on an unprecedented scale, the notion of race-based slavery solidified, intertwining with systems of racism that would endure for centuries. In this way, the decline of indigenous slavery set a precedent for the new era of transatlantic slavery – a state of human bondage that would shape the Americas in unimaginable ways.

This decline in the Americas was orchestrated by a complex interplay of factors, including European colonization, the spread of diseases, and internal changes within indigenous societies. European colonization disrupted the existing systems of indigenous slavery, replacing them with their own forms of forced labour.

Legacy of Indigenous Slavery

Indigenous slavery in the Americas predates European colonization, with various Amerindian tribes practicing slavery among themselves. However, it was the arrival of Europeans that would exacerbate this cruel practice and create the foundation for the transatlantic slave trade. It was a dark period in history, and it left a mark on the Americas that is still felt today.

When Christopher Columbus arrived in the Americas in 1492, he encountered the indigenous peoples of the Caribbean. Rather than celebrating the richness of their culture and establishing peaceful relations, Columbus saw an opportunity for exploitation. He wasted no time in capturing and enslaving these people, forcing them into backbreaking labour.

The Portuguese, Dutch, and English followed in Columbus' footsteps, each establishing their own exploitative colonies throughout the Americas. Indigenous peoples became the targets of their insatiable greed, as their lands were confiscated, their cultures suppressed, and their bodies enslaved. Native communities were decimated, their members forcibly removed from their ancestral lands and sold into slavery.

The legacy of indigenous slavery did not occur in isolation. It would morph into the development of the Atlantic slave trade, which would later see millions of Africans transported across the ocean to fuel the growing demand for labour in the New World. The European colonizers, driven by their insatiable desire for wealth and power, sought to exploit both indigenous peoples and Africans for their own gain.

European colonizers, having witnessed the profitability of slave labour through the enslavement of indigenous peoples, sought new sources of labour when the indigenous population declined due to disease, brutality, and resistance. This led to the tragic displacement of Africans from their homelands, as they became the primary victims of the transatlantic slave trade.

The connections between these two systems are evident in the methods used to subjugate and control enslaved peoples. European colonizers employed similar techniques of dehumanization, coercion, and violence against both Indigenous and African slaves. They sought to strip them of their identities, cultures, and histories to maintain control and domination. In doing so, they perpetuated a cycle of oppression that made an impact on the development of slavery in the Americas.

The implications of this legacy on American slavery cannot be overstated. The transatlantic slave trade, fueled by the lessons learned from indigenous slavery, would shape the economic, social, and political landscape of the New World for centuries to come.

The system of slavery that emerged in the Americas was deeply rooted in racism and White supremacy, born from the womb of indigenous slavery. The practices, ideologies, and institutions that evolved during the era of indigenous slavery provided a blueprint for the oppression and exploitation of Africans. The dehumanization, cultural erasure, and forced labour that characterized indigenous slavery became deeply ingrained in the American psyche, perpetuating a system that denied the humanity of people of African descent.

Reference Poems

The Lamentation of the Enslaved – Book 1
- I am Human

The history of slavery is a painful reminder of humanity's capacity for cruelty and greed. But it is also a testament to the resilience and strength of the oppressed, as they fought tirelessly against their subjugation and contributed immensely to the cultures and societies of the Americas.

In understanding the legacy of indigenous slavery, we must also confront the dark truths of humanity's past. We must acknowledge the interconnectedness of these cruel systems and the ramifications they had on the development of slavery in the Americas. Only through this process of reflection can we recognize, and begin to dismantle, the structures of inequality and injustice that continue impact our world.

The Atlantic Slave Trade

European Expansion

The fifteenth and sixteenth centuries witnessed a fervent wave of European exploration and colonization, driven by a thirst for wealth, power, and prestige. European nations sought to expand their territories, monopolize lucrative trade routes, and extract precious resources. The desire to find new markets and lucrative commodities played a significant role in the expansionist drive. Spices, sugar, coffee, and other luxury goods had become highly prized in European societies, creating a demand that could not be met by existing sources. The New World promised untapped wealth and an endless supply of commodities, which fueled the fires of European expansionism.

Reference Poems

The Lamentation of the Enslaved – Book 1
- The Land Speaks
- Humanity's Mourning

This territorial expansion was not limited to economic objectives; it was also driven by political and strategic considerations. Rivalries among European powers, notably Spain, Portugal, England, France, and the Netherlands, spurred a race for dominance and control over strategic territories. The quest for precious metals, such as gold and silver, often served as a central tenet of these geopolitical ambitions. The conquest of territories like the Americas, Africa, and Asia represented a means for European nations to project their power and secure valuable resources. The colonization of these lands was seen as an extension of European authority and civilization, a grand manifestation of their superiority over these supposedly uncivilized lands and peoples.

The socio-cultural context of Europe during this period also contributed to the growth of the Atlantic slave trade. The development of feudal systems had given way to an emerging capitalist economy, fueled by the burgeoning trade with Asia and the Middle East. This transition led to the restructuring of social relations, as peasants were displaced from their lands and became a dispossessed working class. The labour-intensive agricultural practices in the New World required vast amounts of labour, which Europe could not fully provide, leading to an increased demand for a cheap and abundant workforce.

The transatlantic slave trade emerged as a solution to this pressing need for labour, resulting in one of the most barbaric and dehumanizing systems ever known to humankind. African slaves were considered a suitable labour force due to their perceived physical endurance and their lack of familiarity with the New

World environment. The unfortunate reality was that this institution systematically dehumanized Africans, treating them as commodities to be bought, sold, and exploited for the profits of European powers.

The economic benefits of slavery were immense. Plantations that produced lucrative crops such as tobacco, sugar, and cotton flourished on the backs of enslaved Africans. These products were in high demand in Europe, fueling the growth of industries and enriching everyone but the enslaved. The cheap labour provided by enslaved African allowed for the mass production of these commodities with little to no labour overhead. This in turn contributed to Europe's economic prosperity. The financial gains from slavery were instrumental in financing Europe's industrial revolution and establishing a powerful capitalist system that reverberates in present-day economies.

Politically, the slave trade bolstered European nations as they competed for dominance in the New World. Enslaved Africans were forced to work in mines, plantations, and other industries that extracted and produced valuable resources for their European masters. The wealth generated by the slave-based economies enabled European nations to strengthen their military might, expand their territories, and exert control over vast overseas empires.

However, the negative consequences of this insidious system were far-reaching and devastating. The enslaved Africans endured unimaginable suffering and the loss of their freedoms, cultures, and lives. Families were torn apart, communities decimated, and generations were subjected to the brutalities of bondage. The psychological and emotional scars of enslavement continue to affect the descendants of those who suffered, shaping their experiences and interactions.

The Middle Passage

The conditions aboard the slave ships were nothing short of horrifying. These vessels, often referred to as floating coffins, were crammed with as many human bodies as possible. The captives were stacked together like inanimate cargo. The ship's hold, where these unfortunate souls were confined, was a cramped and suffocating space, where the stench of excrement, sweat, and death hung heavily in the air.

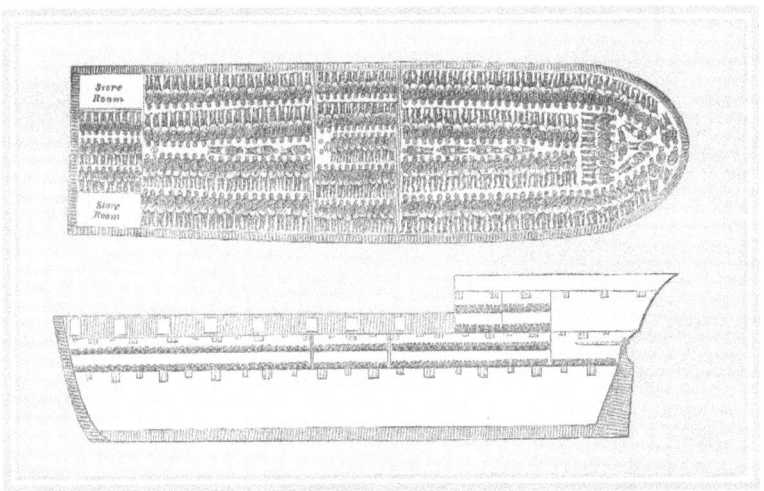

Figure 1- Slave ship - [[File:HOS D326 Decks of a Slave Ship.jpg|HOS D326 Decks of a Slave Ship]] Blake, William O, Public domain, via Wikimedia Commons

Reference Poems

The Lamentation of the Enslaved – Book 1
- The Oceans Breath in His Ear
- Mufa's Despair at Sea
- Into the cauldron
- Mufa's Loss

The captives were subjected to inhumane treatment at the hands of the crew, who viewed them as little more than commodities to be bought, sold, and mercilessly exploited. Shackled and stripped of their dignity, they endured beatings, whippings, and verbal abuse, with no respite from their physical and emotional torment. They were reduced to chattel, stripped of their identities, and treated as mere property to be bought and sold at a whim.

The mortality rates during the Middle Passage were alarmingly high, a fact that underscores the sheer brutality and disregard for human life that characterized this transatlantic trade. From the barracoon, the journey was long, lasting anywhere from six to twelve weeks, during which time the captives were subjected to the most abhorrent conditions imaginable. They were crammed together, with little room to move or breathe, resulting in the spread of diseases such as dysentery, smallpox, and scurvy. Malnutrition was rampant, and the meager rations provided were barely enough to sustain their already weakened bodies.

The lack of sanitation aboard the slave ships only exacerbated the dire conditions. The captives were forced to relieve themselves where they stood, as they had no access to toilets or fresh water. The waste and filth accumulated, becoming a breeding ground for disease and infection. Many captives succumbed to illness and died, their bodies thrown overboard, discarded like refuse. Weakened by their confinement, they were unable to fight off diseases, fading away in the darkness and filth of the ship's hold.

Death was a constant companion aboard these vessels. It is estimated that anywhere from 10 to 25 percent of enslaved Africans perished during the treacherous journey across the Atlantic[ii]. These numbers, although staggering, fall short of capturing the true horror and human suffering that occurred during this period of history.

Reference Poems

The Lamentation of the Enslaved – Book 1
- Winter of His Heart
- I am John Brown
- Stripped
- Helpless Cry

The Middle Passage represented the depths of human cruelty and the devaluation of human life. It was a journey characterized by unspeakable horrors, where enslaved Africans were stripped of their humanity and subjected to unimaginable suffering.

The Middle Passage stands as a stark reminder of the atrocities committed against our fellow human beings, reminding us of how easy it is to justify the subjugation and devastation to our fellow human beings by simply telling ourselves that they are "less than human."

Our collective history is heavy with the weight of these stories and echoes the pain suffered by the millions who were forced to endure the Middle Passage. However, we cannot ignore or forget the resilience and strength displayed by those who survived, their stories a testament to the power of the human spirit in the worst of circumstances.

Unearthing the Mysteries of the Kingdom of Nri

In the Enslaved series, Mufa is a young man from the now lost Kingdom of Nri. This mysterious kingdom, thought to be situated in what is now southeastern Nigeria, remains one of Africa's most intriguing historical enigmas. Nri, also known as the Nri Kingdom, flourished between the 10th and 19th centuries, long before the colonial era reshaped the African continent. Nri played a pivotal role in shaping the cultural and political landscape of the Igbo people, and its legacy endures in the modern-day Igbo culture.

Reference Poems
The Lamentation of the Enslaved – Book 1
- Mufa
- eguzogidela

Although the origins of the Nri Kingdom are shrouded in mystery, its history has been passed down through oral traditions. Legend has it that Eri, the eponymous founder, settled in the area during the 10th century and established a dynasty that would rule for centuries. Eri is considered a divine figure by the Igbo people and is believed to have possessed mystical and supernatural powers.

Nri was unique among African kingdoms in that it was a theocracy, meaning that religious leaders also held considerable political power. The kingdom's political structure was organized around a priest-king known as the "Eze Nri," who served as both the political and spiritual leader. The Eze Nri was believed to have a direct connection with the deities and was responsible for performing religious rituals, mediating conflicts, and maintaining social order.

The Nri Kingdom was not a vast empire but rather a city-state surrounded by satellite towns and villages. The Eze Nri exercised authority over this region, which became known as the "Nri hegemony." The kingdom had a complex system of laws and customs, which emphasized the importance of justice and social harmony.

The influence of the Nri Kingdom extended far beyond its physical borders. It played a pivotal role in shaping Igbo culture and traditions. The Nri hegemony promoted a common Igbo identity and cultural practices. The Igbo people adopted the Nri religious system and institutions, including the belief in a pantheon of deities, divination practices, and various religious rituals. This religious system remains a fundamental part of Igbo spirituality to this day.

The Nri Kingdom also introduced the "Igbo Ukwu" bronze casting, a remarkable artistic tradition that produced intricate sculptures and artifacts. These artifacts, discovered in archaeological excavations, demonstrate the advanced metallurgical skills of the Nri people and reflect their rich cultural heritage.

The Nri Kingdom's power began to wane in the 19th century due to various internal and external factors. European colonialism and the spread of Christianity in the region contributed to the decline of Nri's influence. The kingdom's theocratic system was also challenged by the emergence of other Igbo polities and the British colonial administration.

The last recognized Eze Nri, Eze Nri Ónwu, was deposed by the British in 1911, marking the official end of the Nri Kingdom's political influence. Nevertheless, the cultural legacy of the kingdom continues to resonate within the Igbo community.

Today, the Nri Kingdom's legacy lives on in the traditions and customs of the Igbo people. The Nri religious system remains an integral part of Igbo spirituality, and the Igbo Ukwu bronze artifacts serve as a testament to the kingdom's rich artistic heritage.

Nri is also celebrated for its role in unifying and preserving Igbo culture, helping the Igbo people maintain a distinct identity throughout their history. The kingdom's emphasis on justice and social harmony has left an enduring mark on Igbo society.

The Kingdom of Nri, with its enigmatic origins and unique theocratic system, stands as a testament to the resilience and cultural richness of the Igbo people. Its impact on Igbo culture, religion, and art is still felt in modern Nigeria. The Nri Kingdom's political power may have dissipated over time, but its legacy endures, reminding us of the importance of preserving and honoring the cultural heritage of African civilizations like Nri.

The Triangular Trade

The foundation of the Triangular Trade was the demand for labour in the American colonies. The rapid expansion of European colonies in the Americas necessitated a vast workforce to cultivate crops such as tobacco, sugar, and cotton. The indigenous population, the Amerindians, was initially utilized as a labour force, but factors such as disease and overwork led to their decimation. This created a void that needed to be filled, sparking the transatlantic trade of enslaved Africans.

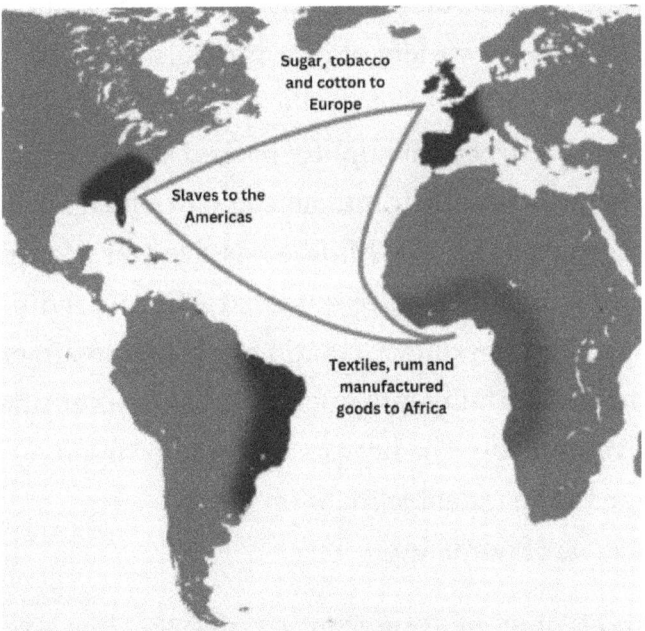

Figure 3 - The Triangular Trade

The Triangular Trade began with European ships sailing to West Africa, laden with goods specifically chosen for trade with African rulers and merchants. These goods included textiles, rum, weapons, and metalware. The Europeans understood the value of these items in establishing diplomatic and economic ties, as well as enticing Africans to trade for captives, who would later be sold as slaves across the Atlantic. The sheer audacity of this exchange, trading goods for human lives, is a testament to the insidiousness and cruelty of the slave trade.

Once the African rulers and merchants had acquired enough slaves, a variety of factors determined the next leg of the Triangular Trade - the Middle Passage. This harrowing journey saw tightly packed ships set sail from West Africa; their human cargo destined for the American colonies. The Middle Passage was a journey plagued with suffering, as enslaved Africans endured cramped and unsanitary conditions, brutal treatment, and a high mortality rate due to disease, malnutrition, and even suicide. The horrors of this treacherous voyage left an indelible mark on the collective conscience of humanity.

Upon reaching the American colonies, the final stage of the Triangular Trade unfolded. The enslaved Africans were sold at auction, with plantation owners and traders eagerly bidding for strong, able-bodied individuals who could endure the grueling labour required to cultivate crops that would be sold in European markets. The transatlantic slave trade created immense human suffering which was traded for a tremendous transformation of the economic landscape of the Americas. The arrival of enslaved Africans contributed greatly to the growth of plantations and industries, enhancing the wealth and power of those who benefited from this system of oppression.

While the Triangular Trade was predominantly associated with the trade of enslaved Africans, it also involved the exchange of goods between Europe and the Americas. Raw materials such as tobacco, sugar, timber, and cotton were shipped from the colonies to Europe, where they fueled the continent's industrial revolution. In return, manufactured goods, textiles, and luxury items flowed from Europe to the Americas, satisfying the growing demand created by the burgeoning population. This dual exchange of goods not only enriched the European powers but also spurred economic development in the American colonies.

The impact of the Triangular Trade extended beyond the realms of commerce. It fostered a deep-seated racism and dehumanization of the African people, perpetuating a narrative of White superiority and Black inferiority that still echoes in society today. The commodification of human lives and the brutal treatment endured by those forced into slavery have left scars that continue to haunt our collective memory.

Without a doubt, the trade itself may have faded into the mists of history, but the ramifications of this system of exploitation and subjugation are still acutely felt. The Triangular Trade was a dark chapter in our shared human story, one that should remind us of the need for advocating for empathy, justice, and reconciliation in our present and future endeavors.

African Kingdoms and the Slave Trade

History cannot ignore the significant role African kingdoms and rulers played in the slave trade. Their motivations for participating, the methods of capturing and selling slaves, and the consequences for African societies are topics that need to be examined.

Reference Poems
The Lamentation of the Enslaved – Book 1
- Mufa
- Eguzogidela
- Helpless Cry

The African continent, with its diverse cultures and kingdoms, had long been engaged in the business of slavery before the arrival of European colonizers. However, it was the lucrative demand for labour in the New World that saw an exponential increase in the scale and brutality of the slave trade.

Yet, we cannot discuss the role of African kingdoms in the slave trade without acknowledging the complex dynamics involved. It is crucial to recognize that not all African rulers – such as the Kingdom of Nri[iii] - willingly participated in this oppressive system. Some resisted, fought against it, or attempted to limit its scope. However, the combination of European guns, goods, and financial incentives proved difficult to resist, ultimately drawing many African rulers into the trade.

The motivations for African kingdoms to engage in the slave trade were varied. Economic gain was certainly a significant factor. The European traders offered enticing rewards such as guns, ammunition, and luxury goods in exchange for slaves. This allowed African rulers to consolidate their power, expand their territories, and gain wealth. Many kingdoms saw the slave trade as an opportunity to acquire valuable goods that could be used to strengthen their military and enhance their political and economic status.

Additionally, some African rulers believed that engagement in the slave trade provided a means of protecting their own people. By participating in the trade, they could ensure that their subjects were not captured and sold by rival kingdoms. This unfortunate and flawed reasoning illustrates the desperate and complex circumstances that led African rulers to justify their involvement in the horrific practice of enslaving fellow Africans.

The methods employed by African kingdoms to capture and sell slaves were also varied. Some kingdoms relied on warfare and raids against neighboring communities to obtain captives. These captives would then be sold to European traders for goods. Other rulers established intricate systems of tribute and taxation, where conquered communities were required to provide a set number of individuals for the slave trade each year. These unfortunate individuals were often chosen based on physical attributes desirable to European buyers, such as strength, youth, and good health.

The consequences of the slave trade for African societies were profound and far-reaching. The widespread capture and sale of able-bodied men and women destabilized communities, disrupted social structures, and led to the loss of valuable contributors to African societies. Young men, often targeted for capture, were taken away from their families and never returned, leaving behind devastated communities and broken families. This loss of labour and potential leaders greatly hindered the development and progress of African societies.

Furthermore, the slave trade introduced firearms to African kingdoms, sparking internecine warfare and conflicts fueled by the desire to acquire captives for trading. This intensification of violence perpetuated a vicious cycle in which kingdoms became both participants and victims of the slave trade.

Moreover, the impact on African culture and identity cannot be underestimated. With the forced migration of enslaved Africans to the Americas, over the course of time cultural practices, traditions, and knowledge were irreversibly lost. The trauma and horrific experiences endured by those forced into slavery echoed through generations, leaving a lasting imprint on the African diaspora.

African kingdoms and rulers played a significant role in the Transatlantic Slave Trade. Motivated by economic gain, self-preservation, or a combination of factors, many kingdoms participated in the capture and sale of their own people. This participation had devastating consequences for African societies, leading to destabilization, loss of labour, and the erosion of cultural identity.

Impact of the Atlantic Slave Trade

The economic, social, and cultural consequences of this transatlantic trade were far-reaching. It left an indelible mark on the lives of countless individuals and societies. In this chapter, we shall analyze the profound impact of the Atlantic slave trade to better understand the magnitude of its effects on the continents of Africa, the Americas and Europe.

Africa: The Heart of the Trade

Africa was the epicenter of the slave trade, and consequently felt the brunt of its negative economic, social, and cultural consequences. Locally, the slave trade disrupted local economies by forcibly extracting able-bodied men and women, who were the backbone of agricultural and labour sectors. The loss of such a sizable portion of the population led to a decline in productivity, causing a ripple effect that trickled down to countless communities. Moreover, the African elites, who acted as intermediaries in the trade, amassed wealth from the exploitation of their own people. The resulting economic disparity and destabilization plagued Africa for generations to come.

Socially, the slave trade ruptured and brutalized traditional African societies, leading to the breakdown of familial bonds, community structures, and cultural norms. Families were torn apart, with loved ones forcibly separated, and sold to different destinations never to be seen again. This shattered the core foundations of African society, leaving deep scars that are still felt today. Additionally, the constant fear of abduction and enslavement created an atmosphere of mistrust and paranoia among African communities, further eroding social cohesion.

Reference Poems

The Lamentation of the Enslaved – Book 1
- The Land Speaks
- Humanity's Mourning
- For the sake of Africa

Culturally, the slave trade had a lasting impact on Africa's cultural landscape. The forced migration of millions of Africans to the Americas meant that their rich heritage and traditions were transplanted onto foreign soil. This involuntary transplantation resulted in the preservation of African customs and languages in the New World, as enslaved Africans sought solace and solidarity in their shared heritage. Despite the immense adversity they faced, African cultural resilience not only survived but thrived, shaping the cultural fabric of the Americas.

The Americas: The Enslaved and the Enslavers

The arrival of African slaves in the Americas marked a turning point in the history of the continent. Economically, slavery became the driving force behind the Americas' agricultural and industrial growth. Africans were subjected to grueling labour in plantations, mines, and factories. The wealth accumulated by slaveholders and their associations laid the foundation for economic prosperity in the Americas, albeit built on the backs of enslaved individuals.

Socially, the institution of slavery created a rigid racial hierarchy that defined every aspect of life in the Americas. Enslaved Africans were systematically dehumanized, denied basic rights, and subjected to unimaginable cruelty. Their lives were heavily regulated, with forced labour dominating their existence, leaving little room for autonomy or personal growth. On the other side of this hierarchy, slave owners and their descendants reveled in privilege and power, perpetuating a system that normalized inequality and oppression.

Culturally, the African diaspora in the Americas wove a tapestry of diverse and vibrant cultures that would eventually influence the development of literature, music, art, religion, and language. From the spiritual traditions of Vodou and Santeria to the rhythm and soul of jazz, blues, and reggae, African cultural contributions would become ubiquitous. Despite enduring unimaginable hardships, enslaved Africans persisted in preserving their unique cultural expressions, safeguarding the essence of their identity.

Europe: The Profiteers and the Consequences

While Africa and the Americas bore the brunt of the Atlantic slave trade, Europe played a pivotal role as the profiteers of this inhumane enterprise. Economically, the slave trade transformed Europe into a global economic powerhouse. The influx of enormous wealth from the trade financed industrialization and bolstered the development of economies. From shipbuilding to finance, Europe's financial markets grew exponentially due to the profits made from the trade, giving rise to a new class of merchant elites who profited from the misery of others.

Socially, the slave trade allowed European societies to justify their superiority, viewing Africans and their descendants as inferior. This racist ideology permeated all aspects of European society, shaping notions of racial superiority and justifying colonization in the name of "civilization." The consequences of this deeply entrenched racism still reverberate today, leaving lasting scars on European society and its treatment of minority populations.

Reference Poems
The Lamentation of the Enslaved – Book 1
- Stripped
- A song of Remembrance
- For the sake of Africa
- Tricked and Stolen

Culturally, the European encounter with Africa and the Americas led to the exchange of ideas, arts, and philosophies that forever altered the cultural landscape of Europe. Through cultural assimilation and appropriation, European artists and thinkers incorporated African and African-American influences into their works, creating a fusion of styles that challenged traditional European norms.

Undoubtedly the Atlantic slave trade's impact on Africa, the Americas, and Europe, rippled through generations and reshaped the course of history. Economically, socially, and culturally, the consequences were profound, with the trade forever altering the trajectory of each continent in turn.

American Slavery

Slavery in Colonial America

The roots of American slavery are grounded in the legal frameworks that were established at its inception. The earliest recorded instance of legalized slavery in colonial America was the establishment of the Jamestown colony in 1607. Here, the Virginia Company introduced indentured servitude, a system that bound individuals to a period of labour in exchange for passage to the New World. However, as time went on, a new precedent took hold. The Virginia General Assembly, motivated by economic gain and racial prejudices, enacted laws in the mid-17th century that made the status of enslaved Africans hereditary, effectively transforming them into property.

One such law was passed in 1662, known as the Partus sequitur ventrem[iv]. It decreed that the child of an enslaved woman would inherit the status of their mother, regardless of the father's identity. This law solidified the institution of slavery, as it ensured that enslaved Africans remained in bondage for generations to come. The legal frameworks surrounding slavery in colonial America were built on a foundation of dehumanization and perpetuated a system deeply rooted in race-based discrimination.

With the legal groundwork firmly in place, labour systems were established to maximize productivity and profitability. One such system was known as the plantation system, which dominated the southern colonies. Enslaved Africans were forced to endure grueling labour on large-scale agricultural estates, primarily cultivating lucrative crops such as tobacco, rice, and indigo. The plantation system relied on a brutal regime of coercion, with overseers and slave drivers ensuring that enslaved Africans remained subservient and productive.

Reference Poems
The Lamentation of the Enslaved – Book 1
- A Song of Remembrance
- My name is Mufa
- Conversation with Massa

The harsh conditions under which enslaved Africans worked were intertwined with the treatment they experienced. The brutal reality of their existence is difficult to comprehend. They were subjected to physical abuse, sexual exploitation, and psychological torture. Families were torn apart through the sale and trade of enslaved Africans, causing immeasurable anguish and trauma that rippled through generations. The treatment of enslaved Africans was marked by a complete disregard for their humanity and a desire to strip them of their dignity.

Indeed, the early presence of slavery in colonial America laid the foundation for a deeply entrenched system of racial oppression. Slavery became an integral part of the very fabric of society, affecting all aspects of colonial life. The economy thrived on the labour of enslaved Africans, with wealth and power concentrated in the hands of slaveholders. The institution of slavery also permeated social and cultural ideologies, reinforcing notions of White supremacy, and perpetuating racial hierarchies that still resonate today.

Plantation Economy

The sun was scorching as she stood in the middle of the vast fields of the plantation. The air was heavy with the scent of sweat and despair, as the relentless heat and the spectre of oppression bore down on her weary soul and exhausted body.

This was the reality of plantation economies in the Americas, a reality built upon the backs of enslaved Africans who were forced into a life of backbreaking labour.

The development of plantation economies in the Americas was a direct result of European colonization and the quest for wealth. It began with the arrival of Christopher Columbus in the New World, and soon after, the establishment of European colonies. The colonial powers sought to exploit the land and its resources, and one of the most efficient ways to achieve this was through agriculture.

Reference Poems
The Lamentation of the Enslaved – Book 1
- I am the Golden Magnolia
- I am Samuel Alford III
- The Golden Magnolia

Agricultural practices in the plantation economies were designed to maximize the yield and profit. The main crops cultivated on these plantations included sugar, coffee, tobacco, rice, indigo, and cotton. Each region had its own specialization, depending on the climate, soil, and other factors. For example, sugar plantations thrived in the Caribbean, while tobacco plantations were more common in North America.

The cultivation of these crops required an immense amount of labour, and this is where the reliance on slave labour came into play. Enslaved Africans were seen as cheap and expendable resources, and thus they became the backbone of the plantation economies. They were captured from their homes, often violently, and transported across the Atlantic Ocean in what would become known as the transatlantic slave trade.

The economic benefits brought by enslaved Africans were immense. Their forced labour ensured that the plantations could produce enormous quantities of crops, which were in high demand in Europe. This influx of goods led to an economic boom in Europe, as the profits from the plantations flowed into the coffers of the colonial powers. The plantation owners amassed great wealth, while the enslaved Africans toiled in unimaginable conditions.

The dehumanizing conditions experienced by enslaved Africans on the plantations were a stark contrast to the opulent lifestyles of their captors. They were crammed into overcrowded and unsanitary living quarters, with minimal access to food, clothing, and healthcare. Their diets consisted of cheap and poorly prepared food, lacking in nutrition. Diseases such as malaria and yellow fever ran rampant. They lived in constant fear of punishment, as the overseers would not hesitate to use violence and brutality to maintain control.

The physical and psychological toll of plantation labour was immense. Enslaved Africans were subjected to long hours of arduous work, often under the scorching sun or in harsh weather conditions. They were expected to work from sunrise to sunset, with truly little respite. This relentless labour took a toll on their bodies, leading to chronic pain, injuries, and premature death.

Beyond the physical hardships, the enslaved Africans also had to endure the dehumanization that came with their status as property. They were stripped of their cultural identities, forcibly separated from their families and communities. Their names were replaced with European ones, further erasing their individuality. They were treated as objects, mere tools to be used and discarded. This dehumanization left a lasting impact on their psyche, as they struggled to maintain a sense of self and dignity amidst the harshness of their reality.

The plantation economies and their reliance on slave labour shaped the social, economic, and cultural landscapes of the Americas. The wealth generated by the plantations fueled the development of cities, infrastructure, and industries. It also perpetuated racial hierarchies and divisions, as the enslaved Africans were seen as inferior and less deserving of basic human rights.

The legacy of plantation economies and slave labour is one of pain and suffering, but it is also a testament to the resilience and strength of those who endured.

Slave Resistance and Revolts

The seeds of resistance were sown soon after the first enslaved Africans were forcibly brought to the Americas. Born out of misery and desperation, the desire for freedom, gave birth to a spirit of resistance that flourished across plantations, forming the driving force behind countless revolts. These acts of defiance ranged from simple acts of rebellion, such as work slowdowns or sabotage, to full-scale uprisings that struck fear into the hearts of their oppressors.

One of the most famous uprisings in the history of the transatlantic slave trade was the Haitian Revolution[v], which erupted on the island of Hispaniola in 1791. Amidst the backdrop of French oppression and the ideals of the French Revolution, African slaves, led by figures like Toussaint Louverture[vi], Jean-Jacques Dessalines[vii], and Dutty Boukman[viii], revolted against their colonial masters. This uprising not only challenged the institution of slavery but also sought the establishment of an independent Black nation. The Haitian Revolution shattered the notion that enslaved Africans were mere chattel and proved that they possessed the ability to organize and fight for their freedom.

Another notable uprising took place in the British colony of Jamaica in 1831-1832. Known as the Baptist War[ix], this revolt was led by Baptist deacon and slave, Samuel Sharpe[x]. Sharpe, driven by the injustices and cruelties he witnessed, organized a peaceful strike of enslaved labourers demanding better working and living conditions. However, when the strike was met with violence and resistance from plantation owners, the situation quickly escalated into a full-scale rebellion. Though the insurrection was eventually crushed, it sent shockwaves throughout the British Empire and prompted the passage of the Slavery Abolition Act in 1833[xi].

The impact of these acts of resistance extended far beyond the immediate goals of liberation. They instilled a newfound sense of empowerment within enslaved Africans, inspiring future generations to stand up against their oppressors. The significance of these acts of defiance can be seen in the legacy of resistance that continued long after the abolition of slavery. From the Maroon communities[xii] in the Americas, where escaped slaves formed their own self-governing societies, to the violent slave revolts in Brazil and the United States, the spark of resistance never died.

The leaders of these revolts played a pivotal role in shaping the course of the fight for freedom. They emerged as iconic figures, symbols of hope and defiance, who led their fellow enslaved Africans in a quest for liberation. Many of them possessed extraordinary leadership qualities, demonstrating not only courage but also intelligence, strategic thinking, and the ability to inspire others. Figures like Nat Turner, who led a rebellion in Virginia in 1831[xiii], and Denmark Vesey, who planned a large-scale revolt in Charleston in 1822[xiv], became legends whose names echoed through time, reminding enslaved Africans and their descendants of the indomitable spirit that resided within them.

Reference Poems
Freedom Bells are Ringing – Book 2
- The Ballad of Nat Turner

The impact of resistance and revolts extended beyond the physical realm. These acts of defiance not only challenged the authority of slaveowners but also laid the groundwork for the broader fight against the institution of slavery itself. They exposed the inherent contradictions of an oppressive system that claimed to uphold the ideals of freedom and liberty while denying these very rights to certain groups of people based on their race. The revolts served as wake-up calls for those who were complicit in the perpetuation of slavery, forcing them to confront the moral and ethical implications of their actions.

Moreover, acts of resistance and revolts shed light on the strength and resilience of the human spirit. They taught future generations that even in the darkest of times, the flame of hope can never be extinguished. These acts of defiance served as a reminder that freedom is worth fighting for, that the yearning for liberation can transcend the boundaries of oppression and ignite a fire within the hearts of those who dare to dream of a better tomorrow.

The struggle for freedom is not a passive one; enslaved Africans refused to accept their dehumanization and resisted with the weapons they had—unity, courage, and an unyielding spirit. Through their acts of defiance, they transformed their bodies, which had been reduced to commodities, into vessels of resistance, reminding us that the price of freedom has always been steep but undeniably worth paying.

Culture and Identity

Resilience and an inner fortitude formed the foundation of the culture and identity of the enslaved. It was this formidable resilience and strength that the enslaved Africans demonstrated in preserving their African traditions, developing new cultural practices, and finding ways to maintain their humanity amidst unimaginable hardship.

Reference Poems
The Lamentation of the Enslaved – Book 1
- Humanity's Mourning
- A song of Remembrance
- I am Tom
- My Name is Mufa
- Conversations with Massa

The preservation of African traditions was a remarkable testament to the enduring spirit of the enslaved Africans. As they were forcibly transported across the Atlantic, their cultural heritage went with them, ingrained deep within their very being. The sacred rituals, storytelling, music, dance, and language of their ancestors found a way to weave its threads into the fabric of their existence in the New World.

Slavery stripped away the physical freedom of the Africans, but it could not dampen their cultural spirits.

The memory of home, of their African homelands, remained vivid within their minds, and they sought solace in recreating aspects of their heritage. Whether through hidden meetings in the secrecy of the night or through communal gatherings in slave quarters, these enslaved Africans found ways to maintain their cultural practices. They held tightly onto their beliefs and traditions, ensuring that they lived beyond the oppressive shackles of enslavement.

In the plantation fields, amidst the grueling labour and unbearable conditions, the enslaved Africans developed new cultural practices as a means of survival. They intertwined elements of African culture with the realities of their new circumstances, resulting in a hybridized culture that was uniquely their own. They adapted their traditional music, such as drumming and call-and-response singing to both communicate covertly and uplift their spirits. They created folk tales that spoke of resilience and resistance, passing them down through generations, serving as a source of inspiration and hope.

The enslaved Africans also modified their traditional cuisine, utilizing the limited ingredients available to them and infusing it with their cultural flavors. These culinary creations became a form of cultural resistance, a way of preserving their heritage while also asserting their autonomy over the meager rations they received. The blend of African ingredients, such as okra and yams, with European staples, like cornmeal and pork, gave birth to a new culinary tradition that still resonates in the Americas today.

Despite the immense brutality and dehumanization, they endured, the enslaved Africans found ways to maintain their humanity. They carved out spaces of autonomy within the constraints of enslavement, clinging onto their dignity. Friendships and familial bonds became vital lifelines, providing support and strength in the face of adversity. The sense of community was paramount, as it fostered not only a sense of belonging but also created a platform for resistance and resilience.

Reference Poems
The Lamentation of the Enslaved – Book 1
- Helpless Cry
- Mufa's Identity
- I am Human
- The Auction I
- The Auction II
- Broken Not Crushed
- A Song of Remembrance
- I am Tom

One of the most significant ways that the enslaved Africans maintained their humanity was through their forms of spiritual expression. Drawing on their African religious beliefs, they infused their practices with new elements, creating syncretic religious traditions that fused African ancestral veneration with Christian spirituality. These new spiritual practices were not only a celebration of their cultural heritage but also a means of resistance, as they provided solace, hope, and a sense of connection to something greater than themselves.

It is evident that though we can view the enslaved Africans as victims of the institution of slavery they were much more. They were individuals who valiantly clung to their cultural roots, developed new practices, and preserved their humanity amidst unfathomable circumstances.

Abolitionist Movements and the Road to Freedom

There are several historical stalwarts that played pivotal roles in the abolitionist movement. People like Frederick Douglass[xv], Harriet Tubman[xvi], and Sojourner Truth[xvii]. These brave souls emerged as beacons of hope, fighting tirelessly to secure the liberation of their enslaved brothers and sisters. Their words resonated with truth and conviction, inspiring countless others to join the cause.

Frederick Douglass, a former slave himself, harnessed the power of his eloquent narratives to expose the horrors of slavery. His autobiography, "Narrative of the Life of Frederick Douglass, an American Slave," shocked readers with its vivid descriptions of the physical and psychological brutality inflicted upon enslaved Africans.

Reference Poems
Freedom Bells are Ringing – Book 2
- Frederick Douglass
- Harriet Tubman
- The Underground Railroad

Harriet Tubman, also known as the "Moses" of her people, was a formidable force who risked her lifetime and again to guide enslaved individuals to freedom through the Underground Railroad. Her daring escapes and audacious rescues defy comprehension. Tubman's unwavering determination and her undeniable courage made her one of the most revered figures in the abolitionist movement.

Sojourner Truth, known for her compelling speeches like "Ain't I a Woman," used her powerful voice to advocate for the rights of enslaved Africans and women. Her words ignited inspired her listeners, rousing them to revolt against the injustices of their time.

The abolitionist movement reached a turning point with the signing of the Emancipation Proclamation by President Abraham Lincoln on January 1, 1863. This declaration declared freedom for all enslaved Africans in Confederate-held territories during the Civil War. Although this monumental step toward liberty marked a pivotal moment in history, the road to freedom remained fraught with challenges and setbacks. The fight did not end with the passing of this proclamation; it merely shifted the battleground to one where the struggle for equality and justice would persist for years to come.

Reference Poems

Freedom Bells are Ringing – Book 2
- The Emancipation Proclamation
- The American Civil War
- Know your place

The impact of the abolitionist movements on American society cannot be overstated. As the fight for freedom gained momentum, a growing number of enslaved Africans found the courage to escape slavery. The Underground Railroad, a clandestine network of safe houses and secret routes, operated by both black and white abolitionists, served as a lifeline for those seeking refuge. This covert operation provided enslaved individuals with a flicker of hope, a glimmer of light in the midst of darkness.

White abolitionists also contributed significantly to the cause, challenging the prevailing notions of their time, and working diligently to dismantle the system of slavery. People like William Lloyd Garrison[xviii], Harriet Beecher Stowe[xix], and John Brown[xx] became instrumental in raising awareness about the atrocities of slavery. Garrison, through his newspaper "The Liberator," fervently called for the immediate abolition of slavery and rallied support for the cause. Stowe's landmark novel, "Uncle Tom's Cabin," depicted the harsh reality of slavery and moved countless readers to question the moral implications of perpetuating such a system. John Brown, although controversial and militant in his approach, sought to incite a slave rebellion with his ill-fated raid on the federal arsenal in Harpers Ferry. While he ultimately failed in his mission, his actions sparked a feverish fervor that would continue to fuel the abolitionist cause.

The American Civil War, which raged from 1861 to 1865, served as the ultimate battleground in the fight over the institution of slavery. With the Confederacy fighting to preserve the practice and the Union standing against it, the outcome of this bloody conflict would determine the fate of enslaved Africans. The war's end in 1865 marked a monumental victory for the abolitionist movement as the Thirteenth Amendment was ratified, officially abolishing slavery throughout the United States.

Reference Poems

Freedom Bells are Ringing – Book 2
- The Great Awakening
- Robert Smalls
- 40 Acres
- …And a mule

Yet, the road to freedom was not without its challenges, even after the Emancipation Proclamation and the ratification of the Thirteenth Amendment. The aftermath of Emancipation presented a host of social, economic, and political obstacles for newly freed Africans. The lack of education, limited job opportunities, and continued racial discrimination hindered their progress toward true freedom and equality.

The rise of abolitionist movements and the eventual road to freedom for enslaved Africans in the Americas was a story of resilience, courage, and unwavering determination. The efforts of key figures like Frederick Douglass, Harriet Tubman, and Sojourner Truth, along with the occurrence of noteworthy events such as the Emancipation Proclamation and the American Civil War, transformed American society and challenged the fabric of slavery.

While much work still remained to be done, the abolitionist movements were an essential catalyst for change, inspiring a generation to question the injustices of their time.

The Legacy of American Slavery

Jim Crow Era and Segregation

The Jim Crow era, which spanned roughly from the late 19th century to the mid-20th century, saw the implementation of a series of laws and practices that enforced racial segregation and discrimination against African Americans. These laws, named after a minstrel, show character who epitomized racial stereotypes, imposed a rigid and oppressive racial hierarchy on society. The overarching aim was to maintain white supremacy and control every facet of the lives of African Americans.

Reference Poems
Freedom Bells are Ringing – Book 2
- Free Indeed
- Slave Society or Society with Slaves
- What If
- The Black Codes
- Welcome my Apprentice
- Slavery by another name

On a social level, Jim Crow laws perpetuated a culture deeply rooted in racism, promoting the idea of white superiority and black inferiority. African Americans were subjected to constant humiliation, segregation, and degradation, as they were forced to use separate facilities such as schools, restrooms, and public transportation. The "separate but equal" doctrine, upheld by the Supreme Court in the landmark case Plessy v. Ferguson in 1896[xxi], reinforced the belief that segregation was acceptable as long as the facilities designated for African Americans were deemed equal in quality to those for whites. However, in reality, the facilities provided to African Americans were often woefully inadequate, with overcrowded and underfunded schools, dilapidated infrastructure, and limited access to essential services.

Reference Poems
Freedom Bells are Ringing – Book 2
- Jim Crow
- Who was Jim Crow
- Segregation De Jure
- Plessy v. Ferguson

Politically, African Americans faced significant barriers to participation in the democratic process. Poll taxes, literacy tests, and other discriminatory measures were instituted to prevent African Americans from exercising their right to vote. Grandfather clauses[xxii] and other cunning legal maneuvers effectively excluded black voters while ensuring that white voters were not affected. The suppression of the African American vote served as a means of maintaining white political dominance and subjugating the black population.

The economic consequences of this era were equally devastating for African Americans. Jim Crow laws reinforced economic disparities between Whites and Blacks, leaving African Americans marginalized and relegated to the lowest rungs of society. Employment opportunities for African Americans were limited, with many jobs reserved exclusively for White individuals. Arrangements such as sharecropping, which emerged after the abolition of slavery, kept African American farmers mired in debt and dependent on white landowners. The limited access to quality education, coupled with employment discrimination, meant that upward mobility for African Americans remained elusive.

Reference Poems
Freedom Bells are Ringing – Book 2
- Free Indeed
- The Foster Family
- Segregation Du Jure
- Northern Jim Crow

These social, political, and economic consequences had far-reaching effects on African American communities. Families were torn apart as generations faced limited opportunities for advancement and struggled to escape the cycle of poverty. The psychological toll of living under constant discrimination and marginalization cannot be overstated. African Americans were forced to navigate a society that constantly reminded them of their supposed inferiority, undermining their self-worth and sense of belonging.

Resisting the oppressive system of Jim Crow laws and racial segregation, African Americans embarked on a brave and determined quest for justice and equality. Leaders like Rosa Parks, Martin Luther King Jr., and countless others became torchbearers for the civil rights movement, challenging discriminatory policies and demanding change. Boycotts, sit-ins, and protests became powerful tools for mobilizing communities and bringing attention to the systemic injustices faced by African Americans.

The ultimate legacy of the Jim Crow era and racial segregation is a testament to both the resilience and the ongoing struggle for African Americans to secure equal rights and opportunities. It is a reminder that the fight for justice and equality is an ongoing battle, one that requires vigilance, understanding, and a willingness to confront the deeply entrenched systems of racism that persist in our society.

Civil Rights Movement

The seeds of the Civil Rights Movement were sown long before its prominent emergence in the 1950s and 1960s. Deeply rooted in the history of slavery and its aftermath, the fight for civil rights had been brewing for centuries. It was a response to the pervasive discrimination and systemic oppression that African Americans faced in virtually every aspect of their lives.

The events that unfolded during the Civil Rights Movement, could be said to have begun with the landmark decision of Brown v. Board of Education in 1954[xxiii]. This Supreme Court ruling declared that segregation in public schools was unconstitutional, striking a crucial blow to the prevailing "separate but equal" doctrine. This milestone decision set the stage for the years of activism and protest that were to follow.

Reference Poems
Freedom Bells are Ringing – Book 2
- Plessy v Ferguson
- Brown v Board of Education

One of the most notable figures in the Civil Rights Movement was Rosa Parks[xxiv], a courageous woman who refused to give up her seat to a white passenger on a Montgomery, Alabama bus in 1955. This simple act of resistance sparked the Montgomery Bus Boycott[xxv], a pivotal moment in the history of the movement. Led by a young Reverend Martin Luther King Jr.[xxvi], the boycott lasted for over a year and ultimately resulted in the desegregation of Montgomery's bus system.

Reference Poems
Freedom Bells are Ringing – Book 2
- Lucille Times
- Rosa Parks
- Her name is Ruby Bridges
- The Legend of Ruby Bridges
- Martin Luther King Jr.
- Malcolm X
- Martin Luther King Jr. and Malcolm X

The sit-ins that took place during the early 1960s were another defining aspect of the movement. African American students, inspired by the success of the Montgomery Bus Boycott, began staging peaceful protests at segregated lunch counters and restaurants in the South. These sit-ins not only challenged the deeply ingrained beliefs and practices of segregation but also served as a powerful catalyst for further civil rights activism.

In 1963, the nation witnessed the watershed moment of the March on Washington for Jobs and Freedom[xxvii].

This historic event brought together hundreds of thousands of individuals from all levels of society, united in their demand for equality and justice. It was during this march that Dr. Martin Luther King Jr. delivered his iconic "I Have a Dream[xxviii]" speech, which eloquently articulated the aspirations of the entire movement.

The Civil Rights Act of 1964[xxix] was a significant legislative achievement that emerged as a direct result of the relentless efforts of civil rights activists. This ground-breaking law prohibited racial segregation in public places and outlawed discrimination in employment based on race, colour, religion, sex, or national origin. It was a profound step forward in the fight for racial equality, but it also highlighted the ongoing challenges that lay ahead.

One of the key figures in the fight for voting rights was none other than John Lewis[xxx], an influential civil rights leader and congressman who dedicated his life to the pursuit of equality. The Selma to Montgomery marches in 1965[xxxi], led by Lewis and other activists, aimed to draw attention to the systematic disenfranchisement of African American voters in the South. These marches were met with brutal violence from law enforcement, but they ultimately led to the passage of the Voting Rights Act of 1965[xxxii].

Reference Poems
Freedom Bells are Ringing – Book 2
- No vote, No voice
- Mamie Till Mobley
- Emmett Till
- Emmett's Funeral
- The Negro Motorist Green Book
- The Ku Klux Klan
- Freedom Fighters

The Civil Rights Movement was not without its setbacks and tragedies. The assassination of Medgar Evers[xxxiii] in 1963 and the murder of three civil rights activists, James Chaney, Andrew Goodman, and Michael Schwerner[xxxiv], during the Freedom Summer of 1964 were stark reminders of the intense resistance and hatred that characterized this turbulent era.

However, amidst the challenges and sacrifices, the Civil Rights Movement achieved significant breakthroughs. It paved the way for the landmark case of Loving v. Virginia[xxxv] in 1967, which invalidated laws prohibiting interracial marriage. It also served as a powerful inspiration for other marginalized groups, igniting their own movements for equality and justice.

Reference Poems

Freedom Bells are Ringing – Book 2
- The Blinding of Isaac Woodward
- Hugh Burnett
- Viola Desmond
- Who is the real enemy

The legacy of the Civil Rights Movement reverberates throughout our nation's history. It is a testament to the power of ordinary individuals to effect change and to the resilience of the human spirit in the face of adversity.

Systemic Racism and Structural Inequality

The transatlantic slave trade, which flourished from the 16th to the 19th century, laid the foundation for the racial hierarchy that continues to define our societies. Africans were forcibly taken from their homelands, transported across the Atlantic Ocean, and sold as chattel slaves in the Americas, including the Caribbean and the United States. This dehumanizing trade formed the bedrock of systemic racism, as it not only commodified human beings but also established racial superiority and inferiority based on skin colour.

The subsequent period of colonization further entrenched this racial hierarchy, as European powers sought to exploit the resources and labour of the lands they occupied. Indigenous peoples in the Americas were subjugated, dispossessed of their lands, and subjected to forced labour. They too became victims of systemic racism, facing marginalization, cultural erasure, and the loss of their languages and traditions. The legacies of slavery and colonization continue to reverberate in contemporary society, perpetuating inequity, and injustice.

One area in which systemic racism and structural inequality are particularly evident is education. Access to quality education has long been unevenly distributed, with marginalized communities often receiving subpar resources and support. Inadequate funding, outdated infrastructure, and limited access to technology are just some of the barriers faced by racial and ethnic minority students. This inequality in education perpetuates the cycle of disadvantage, making it difficult for these students to break free from the traps of poverty and limited opportunities.

Reference Poems

Hidden In Plain Sight – Book 3
- Setting the stage
- Abolition: Disappeared Promises
- Good news: Slavery's Abolished
- ...No! You're wrong
- A dream

Furthermore, the portrayal of historical events and narratives in educational curricula often perpetuates stereotypes and reinforces racial biases. Eurocentric perspectives dominate the teaching of history, leaving little room for the stories and contributions of marginalized groups. This erasure of diverse voices not only limits students' understanding of the complexities of the past but also perpetuates a distorted worldview that maintains systemic racism.

Another area deeply affected by systemic racism and structural inequality was employment. Racial and ethnic minorities face significant barriers in accessing and advancing in the labour market. Discrimination during the hiring process, limited opportunities for promotion, and wage disparities are just some of the challenges experienced by marginalized communities. The persistently higher unemployment rates among these groups reflected, not only individual bias but also systemic barriers, that hindered equal opportunities for economic prosperity.

The criminal justice system was yet another arena where the enduring presence of systemic racism and structural inequality is shockingly apparent. People of colour, particularly Black individuals, are disproportionately represented in prisons and subjected to harsher punishments compared to their White counterparts for similar offenses. This racial bias extended beyond the courtroom, permeating all stages of the criminal justice system. Police brutality and racial profiling further compounded these injustices, eroding trust between law enforcement agencies and marginalized communities.

Reference Poems

Hidden In Plain Sight – Book 3
- One Bad Apple
- Break the cycle
- The Black in BIPOC
- The Indigenous in BIPOC
- The People of Colour in BIPOC

The manifestation of systemic racism and structural inequality in other areas of life, such as healthcare, housing, and political representation, cannot be ignored either. Racial and ethnic minorities often face disparities in access to quality healthcare, leading to worse health outcomes and higher mortality rates. Housing discrimination continues to limit affordable and safe housing options for marginalized communities, perpetuating segregation, and inequalities. Additionally, racial, and ethnic minority groups are underrepresented in positions of political power, leading to a lack of diverse perspectives, and diminishing the voice of these communities in shaping policies that directly affect them.

Reference Poems

Hidden In Plain Sight – Book 3
- Doctor Racist
- Judge Racist
- Officer Racist
- Bora a Racist
- Micro Aggression

To dismantle systemic racism and address structural inequality, a multilayered approach is required. It begins with acknowledging the historical injustices that have shaped our societies and reflecting on our own biases and privileges.

Education plays a crucial role in this process, with curricula that encompass a diverse range of voices, perspectives, and histories. Adequate funding and targeted support should be provided to schools in marginalized communities to ensure equal access to quality education.

In the realm of employment, proactive measures must be implemented to eliminate discriminatory practices and promote diversity and inclusion. Employers should be held accountable for creating equitable workplaces that value and uplift individuals from all racial and ethnic backgrounds.

Within criminal justice, serious efforts must be taken to address racial bias and reform a system that disproportionately targets people of colour. Police departments should implement comprehensive training programs aimed at combating implicit bias, ensuring fair and unbiased policing. The implementation of sentencing reform is also crucial in addressing the disproportionate incarceration rates faced by racial and ethnic minorities.

Addressing disparities in healthcare, housing, and political representation requires a comprehensive approach that prioritizes equitable access and opportunities for marginalized communities. Healthcare policies and programs should be designed to address the specific needs of different populations and reduce healthcare disparities. Affirmative action initiatives were used to help address housing discrimination and promote affordable and safe housing options for marginalized communities. However, the enduring presence of systemic racism and structural inequality in contemporary society is a stark reminder of the historical injustices perpetuated against marginalized communities.

Education, employment, criminal justice, and other areas of life continue to be affected by these issues. It is imperative that we confront and dismantle systemic barriers, ensuring equal access and opportunities for all. Only by doing so can we move toward a more equitable and just society, where every individual is afforded the dignity and respect, they deserve.

Reparations and Restorative Justice

The transatlantic slave trade, which spanned over four centuries, claimed the lives and livelihoods of millions of individuals who were forcibly taken from their homes, families, and communities. They were subjected to brutal and inhumane treatment, facing physical, emotional, and psychological abuse.

The legacy of slavery reverberates through generations, leaving a lingering impact on the descendants of those who endured such unimaginable horrors. It has shaped societal structures and systems that perpetuate discrimination, inequality, and injustice. Reparations, therefore, aim to address these historical wrongs, seeking to heal wounds that have festered for far too long.

However, the notion of reparations is far from a simple one. It sparks passionate debates and ignites intense discussions on the most effective means of rectifying past injustices. Some argue for monetary compensation, seeking to provide tangible restitution for the economic exploitation and loss suffered by enslaved Africans and their descendants. Others advocate for social programs and initiatives that aim to uplift marginalized communities, providing access to education, healthcare, housing, and employment opportunities.

These differing approaches to reparations highlight the complexities inherent in seeking justice for historical wrongs. It is not merely a matter of allocating funds or implementing policies; it is a profound reckoning with the systemic structures that perpetuate inequality and marginalization. It requires a fundamental shift in societal consciousness, challenging ingrained biases and prejudices that have been deeply ingrained over generations.

But beyond the practical considerations of reparations lies the importance of acknowledging historical injustices. It is a fundamental aspect of restorative justice, recognizing the pain and suffering endured by enslaved Africans and ensuring that their story is acknowledged and remembered. Only by actively confronting the horrors of the past can we hope to create a more just and equitable future.

Moreover, the concept of restorative justice emphasizes the importance of community healing. It is not enough to simply provide reparations on an individual basis; there must be a collective effort to address the systemic issues that perpetuate inequality. This entails investing in education and awareness programs that challenge the prevailing narratives surrounding slavery, dismantling the racial hierarchies that continue to dominate our societies.

Reference Poems

Hidden In Plain Sight – Book 3
- A Strange Inconsistency
- Plantation Capitalism: A Bitter Sugar Addiction
- Amassing Wealth in not Common Wealth

In this pursuit of restorative justice, it is crucial to engage in an open and honest dialogue. This means confronting uncomfortable truths, acknowledging privilege, and actively seeking to rectify the historical injustices that have shaped our world. It requires collaboration, empathy, and a commitment to dismantling the oppressive structures that have perpetuated inequality for far too long.

The significance of reparations and restorative justice lies in their potential to transform our society. It is an opportunity to confront our shared history, to acknowledge the pain and suffering endured by enslaved Africans, and to work towards a future where equality, justice, and opportunity are afforded to all. It is a call to action, a reminder that our past informs our present, but it does not dictate our future. By embracing reparations and restorative justice, we not only acknowledge the profound injustices of the past, but we lay the groundwork for a more equitable and compassionate world.

Towards a More Just Future

It is important to note that progress towards racial justice and equality has not been linear. Rather, it has been a tumultuous journey, marked by moments of tremendous triumph and profound disappointment.

The 1800s marked a significant turning point in the fight for racial justice, as it witnessed the abolition of the transatlantic slave trade. The work of activists like William Wilberforce and Harriet Tubman brought the horrors of slavery to the forefront of public consciousness. With the Emancipation Proclamation in the United States in 1863, millions of enslaved Africans were freed, but the scars of slavery remained. The racial hierarchy that had been entrenched by centuries of enslavement did not simply disappear overnight; it required a tireless effort to dismantle.

Moving into the twentieth century, the Civil Rights Movement emerged as a beacon of hope in the fight for racial justice and equality. Led by remarkable figures such as Malcolm X, Martin Luther King Jr. and Rosa Parks, this movement challenged the legitimacy of racial discrimination and segregation. Through nonviolent protests, sit-ins, and grassroots organizing, African Americans fought for their rights and demanded justice. The landmark passage of the Civil

Rights Act of 1964[xxxvi] and the Voting Rights Act of 1965[xxxvii] brought about significant legal protections against racial discrimination. These pivotal moments in history paved the way for progress towards racial equality.

Reference Poems

Freedom Bells are Ringing – Book 2
- Malcolm X
- Martin Luther King Jr.
- The Great Debate II
- Martin Luther King Jr and Malcolm X

However, we must acknowledge the tremendous amount of work that remains. Despite the achievements of the Civil Rights Movement, systemic racism has persisted in our society. Economic disparities, educational inequities, and racial profiling continue to hamper the progress towards racial justice. The fight for racial equality is not just about changing laws; it is about dismantling the deeply ingrained biases and prejudices that have shaped our society.

Education plays a pivotal role in this ongoing struggle. By learning about the historical context of racial injustice, we can gain a deeper understanding of its complexities. Education equips us with the knowledge to challenge misconceptions, challenge inequality, and work towards a more just society. It is through education that we can empower individuals to act and create change.

Activism is another crucial element in the fight for racial justice and equality. Activists throughout history have played a pivotal role in challenging the status quo and demanding accountability. From the civil rights activists of the past to the Black Lives Matter movement of today, activists have continuously pushed for change. Through demonstrations, protests, and advocacy, their collective efforts have forced society to confront its biases and work towards a more just future.

Reference Poems
Hidden In Plain Sight – Book 3
- Still Tricked – Justice is MIA
- Shades
- Black Lives Matter Too

However, the struggle for racial justice should not be shouldered by activists alone. Collective efforts are essential in creating lasting change. It is through collective action that individuals from divergent backgrounds and perspectives can come together to challenge the inequalities that plague our society.

When we stand in solidarity with marginalized communities, we can help by amplifying their voices and working together to create a future where racial equality is a reality.

Resistance and Abolition

Revolts and Uprisings

Throughout different regions and time periods, the enslaved fought against their oppressors with a fierce determination and an unyielding spirit. One of the earliest recorded slave revolts took place in the year 1522, on the island of Hispaniola in the Caribbean. This uprising ignited a flame of resistance that would burn throughout the centuries.

However, it was in the 18th and 19th centuries that slave revolts and uprisings reached their zenith. The harsh conditions of plantation life and the relentless brutality of the slave system pushed the enslaved to their breaking point. In 1791, on the island of Saint-Domingue[xxxviii] (now known as Haiti), one of the most significant and successful slave revolts in history took place. Known as the Haitian Revolution, this uprising was led by figures like François-Dominique Toussaint Louverture and Jean-Jacques Dessalines. Through a combination of guerrilla warfare tactics and sheer determination, the enslaved population of Haiti achieved their freedom, creating the first independent Black nation in the Western Hemisphere.

But the struggle for freedom did not end there. Across the Atlantic, another uprising was taking place. In 1831, in the southern United States, a slave named Nat

Turner led a rebellion in Virginia. This revolt, often referred to as Nat Turner's Rebellion, sent shockwaves throughout the South. With a deep religious conviction and a desire for emancipation, Turner and his followers rose up against their oppressors, carrying out a series of brutal and strategic attacks. Although the rebellion was quelled, it left an indelible mark on the consciousness of White slaveholders, leading to even harsher laws against the enslaved and reinforcing the institution of slavery.

Moving further across the globe, we come to the Caribbean Island of Jamaica in the year 1831. Here, another significant uprising unfolded, known as the Baptist War or the Christmas Rebellion. Led by a Baptist deacon named Sam Sharpe, this rebellion was fueled by both religious and political motivations. The enslaved population, inspired by the abolitionist movement and the desire for freedom, launched a widespread revolt that lasted for 10 days. While the rebellion was suppressed, its impact cannot be underestimated. The Baptist War brought the horrors of slavery to the forefront of public consciousness and galvanized the abolitionist movement in Britain.

These are just a few examples of the many slave revolts and uprisings that have occurred throughout history. Each rebellion had its own unique leaders and consequences, but they all shared a common goal: the liberation of the enslaved from the chains of bondage. These acts of resistance were not only a response to physical brutality but also a rejection of the dehumanization and systematic oppression that defined the institution of slavery.

The repercussions of these slave revolts and uprisings were far-reaching. On one hand, they struck fear into the hearts of the slaveholders, who saw their dominant power structure challenged by the enslaved. This fear led to increased violence and repression against the enslaved population, as slaveholders sought to maintain control over those they deemed as property. On the other hand, these acts of resistance provided inspiration and hope for future generations of the oppressed. They laid the groundwork for the abolitionist movement and paved the way for the eventual dismantling of the slave system.

Abolitionist Movements

Abolitionist movements began to gain momentum during the late 18th and early 19th centuries. As the horrors of the transatlantic slave trade became increasingly exposed, various individuals and organizations rose to challenge and overthrow this abhorrent system.

One of the earliest and most influential figures in the abolitionist movement was Olaudah Equiano[xxxix], a former slave himself who vividly recounted his experiences in his autobiography, "The Interesting Narrative of the Life of Olaudah Equiano". Published in 1789, Equiano's book became a powerful tool in raising awareness about the cruelty and inhumanity of slavery. His eloquent writing and personal account of the transatlantic voyage ignited public outrage, serving as a catalyst for the abolitionist cause.

The late 18th and early 19th centuries saw the emergence of several key figures who dedicated their lives to the abolitionist movement. One such individual was William Wilberforce[xl], a British politician and philanthropist. Wilberforce tirelessly campaigned against the transatlantic slave trade and was instrumental in the passing of the Slave Trade Act of 1807[xli] in Britain, which prohibited British ships from engaging in the slave trade. It was a significant step forward, though the abolition of slavery itself would only come later.

Another prominent figure was Harriet Beecher Stowe[xlii], an American writer whose novel, "Uncle Tom's Cabin", published in 1852, had a profound impact on the abolitionist movement. The novel presented a damning portrayal of the realities of slavery and humanized enslaved individuals in a way that deeply resonated with readers. "Uncle Tom's Cabin" sparked widespread debate and further strengthened the abolitionist cause, both in the United States and abroad.

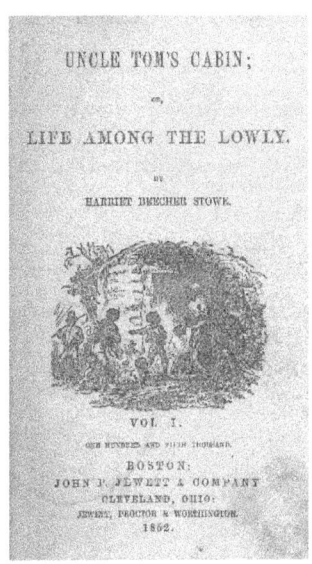

Figure 4 - Uncle Tom's Cabin by Harriet Beecher Stowe https://muarchives.missouri.edu/images/exh_libraries/LE-SpecUncleTomsCabinLarge300res.jpg

In addition to these individual advocates, various organizations played a significant role in the fight against slavery. One such organization was the British and Foreign Anti-Slavery Society[xliii], founded in 1839. This organization brought together individuals from divergent backgrounds and nations who shared a common goal: the eradication of slavery. Through their campaigns, speeches, and publications, the society played a pivotal role in shaping public opinion and pressuring governments to act against the slave trade.

Similarly, in the United States, the American Anti-Slavery Society emerged as a major force in the abolitionist movement. Formed in 1833, the society advocated for immediate emancipation and the abolition of slavery throughout the country. Led by figures such as William Lloyd Garrison and Frederick Douglass, the American Anti-Slavery Society organized public lectures, distributed anti-slavery literature, and actively supported efforts to assist escaped slaves on the Underground Railroad.

The strategies employed by these abolitionist movements varied, reflecting the different contexts in which they operated. Many campaigners focused on raising public awareness and changing public opinion through lectures, pamphlets, and newspapers. The power of the written word cannot be underestimated in this fight, as it helped to expose and document the suffering endured by enslaved individuals.

Moreover, direct action and civil disobedience were common tactics employed by abolitionists. They organized boycotts of slave-produced goods, held public protests, and even engaged in acts of sabotage against the slave trade infrastructure. Escaped slaves often joined these movements and shared their harrowing narratives, adding further weight to the call for abolition.

The abolitionist movements also found support within religious communities. Many religious leaders, such as Quakers and members of the Evangelical movement, were among the earliest and most fervent abolitionists. They argued that slavery was a moral evil and antithetical to the principles of Christianity. The strong religious conviction behind the abolitionist cause helped to galvanize support and added a moral imperative to the fight against slavery.

The development of abolitionist movements around the world marked a turning point in human history. For the first time, concerted efforts were made to challenge the institution of slavery and advocate for the rights and freedom of enslaved individuals. The dedication and bravery of the key figures, as well as the organizations and strategies employed, played a crucial role in eventually bringing about the end of the transatlantic slave trade.

Underground Railroad and Freedom Networks

The Underground Railroad, despite its name, was not a physical network nor a railroad system underground. Rather, it was a clandestine network of individuals, both Black and White, who aided escaped slaves seeking freedom. This covert system operated during the 18th and 19th centuries, mainly in the United States and Canada, and extended its reach into the broader North American continent.

Reference Poems

Freedom Bells are Ringing – Book 2
- The Underground Railroad
- The Ballad of Nat Turner
- Harriet Tubman

The routes of the Underground Railroad were vast and varied, with key locations serving as safe havens for escaping slaves. These routes comprised a network of secret hiding places, known as "stations," which were often the homes or establishments of sympathetic individuals who were willing to harbor escaped slaves. These stations formed a series of communication points where information, resources, and, most importantly, freedom were exchanged. The journey from the South to the North was treacherous, fraught with danger and uncertainty. Yet, the Underground Railroad provided a glimmer of hope for those yearning for liberation.

With each station, a new chapter was written in the story of freedom. From the perilous crossings of the Ohio River to the hidden refuge of the Quaker farms, the Underground Railroad was a lifeline for many enslaved individuals seeking to break the chains of bondage.

The methods employed by those involved in the Underground Railroad were as diverse and innovative as the people themselves. Often, a network of "conductors," consisting of sympathetic individuals of both races, would guide escaping slaves from one station to another. They would rely on a system of secret codes and signals, such as songs or lanterns, to communicate and navigate through treacherous territories. The response to these signals was critical, as they signaled the safety or danger of the journey. These intricacies ensured the successful passage of numerous enslaved individuals towards freedom.

Abolitionists played a pivotal role in the Underground Railroad and other freedom networks. They were the backbone of this covert operation, tirelessly working to dismantle the institution of slavery and offer support to those who sought liberation. These brave individuals risked their lives and faced severe consequences for their actions, as aiding and abetting runaway slaves was illegal.

Names and stories that have inspired both admiration and awe include figures such as Harriet Tubman who dedicated her life to leading enslaved individuals to freedom. Tubman made multiple dangerous trips back into the South, risking her life to rescue her family and countless others. Her unwavering determination and strength of spirit continue to inspire generations today.

Other notable abolitionists, such as William Still[xliv] and Levi Coffin[xlv], played significant roles in the success of the Underground Railroad. Still, an African American abolitionist, meticulously documented the stories of escaped slaves and provided invaluable resources for future operations. Coffin, a Quaker, opened his home as a station and is estimated to have aided approximately three thousand fleeing individuals on their path to freedom.

Without the commitment and courage of these abolitionists and countless others, the Underground Railroad and other freedom networks would not have thrived. Their determination to eradicate slavery and uphold the values of justice and equality transformed what seemed like an insurmountable task into a reality.

The Underground Railroad and other freedom networks were crucial lifelines for enslaved individuals seeking freedom. The routes and methods employed in these networks were as diverse as the individuals who devoted their lives to shaping a future where freedom was a birthright and not a luxury. The abolitionists, both Black and White, who risked everything to aid in this cause, were the heroes behind these networks.

International Abolition and Diplomacy

The journey towards international abolition commenced with the signing of the Treaty of Madrid in 1750[xlvi]. This treaty, negotiated between Britain and Spain, aimed to suppress the illicit slave trade in the Atlantic. Its provisions included tightening regulations on the transport of enslaved Africans, establishing an inspection system for slave ships, and promoting the mutual agreement that both nations had a moral obligation to provide assistance to any captured illicit slavers. While the treaty primarily focused on the British and Spanish colonies, it marked the beginning of diplomatic efforts to address the issue on an international scale.

The next significant milestone came in 1794, with the signing of the Dutch-American Treaty of Amity and Commerce[xlvii]. This ground-breaking agreement, negotiated between the United States and the Netherlands, stipulated that both nations would not participate in the international slave trade, setting a precedent for future diplomatic efforts in the fight against slavery.

The next significant development in international abolition was the 1815 Congress of Vienna[xlviii], which aimed to restore stability in Europe following the

Napoleonic Wars. During this congress, several European powers, including Britain and France, voiced their commitment to ending the transatlantic slave trade. This diplomatic victory laid the groundwork for the subsequent 1817 Treaty of London[xlix], which further reinforced the international ban on the slave trade. This treaty, signed by Britain, France, the Netherlands, Portugal, Spain, and Sweden, represented a collective effort to combat the slave trade by implementing joint naval patrols to intercept and suppress slave ships.

These treaties and conventions were undoubtedly important in galvanizing the global movement against slavery. However, it is essential to acknowledge the critical role played by individuals and grassroots organizations. For example, we cannot ignore the tireless efforts of abolitionists like William Wilberforce, Thomas Clarkson, and Frederick Douglass, who tirelessly campaigned for the end of the slave trade and the emancipation of enslaved people. Their advocacy, speeches, and writings helped raise awareness, challenging public opinion and lending momentum to the international abolition movement.

These abolitionists often found themselves negotiating with governments and diplomats, employing diplomacy as a means of achieving their objectives. By engaging with leaders, politicians, and diplomats, they attempted to sway public opinion and secure legislative measures against the slave trade. Their efforts solidified the idea that diplomacy was a critical tool in the fight against slavery, proving that moral conviction and intellectual persuasion were powerful forces that could bring about change.

The impact of these treaties, conventions, and the global movement against slavery cannot be overstated. These diplomatic endeavors created an international framework that held nations accountable for their participation in the transatlantic slave trade. This framework not only elevated the status of the abolition movement but also insisted on the moral imperative of ending slavery.

Moreover, the international abolition movement united individuals and organizations from diverse backgrounds, transcending national boundaries to form a collective voice against the institution of slavery. This solidarity fostered a sense of shared purpose and created a network of support that extended far beyond individual countries or regions.

Additionally, the international movement against slavery played a significant role in shaping public opinion, challenging the legitimacy of an institution that had been deeply ingrained in society for centuries.

Through literature, pamphlets, speeches, and visual depictions, abolitionists humanized enslaved Africans, highlighting their suffering, and advocating for their rights. These efforts transcended geographical boundaries, reaching individuals in all corners of the world and inspiring empathy and action.

The international efforts towards abolition and the role of diplomacy in ending the slave trade were pivotal in the fight for liberation. From the signing of treaties and conventions to the tireless advocacy of abolitionists, these endeavors galvanized a global movement against slavery. These diplomatic endeavors laid the foundation for future victories in the long and arduous road to freedom for the enslaved.

Legacy of Resistance and Abolition

The legacy of resistance against slavery can be traced back to the very beginnings of the transatlantic slave trade. From the moment Africans were forcibly taken from their homes and brought to the Americas, they began resisting in numerous ways. Whether it was through acts of rebellion, escape, or the preservation of their cultural heritage, enslaved Africans refused to accept their dehumanization and fought for their rights.

One of the most significant forms of resistance was rebellion. Throughout the years, numerous slave revolts occurred on plantations and in cities across the Americas. These acts of defiance were often met with brutal repression, but they sent a powerful message to the slaveholders that their control was not absolute.

Escape was another form of resistance that displayed the determination and resourcefulness of the enslaved. The Underground Railroad, a network of secret routes and safe houses, allowed thousands of enslaved individuals to escape to free states or to Canada.

While rebellion and escape were tangible acts of resistance, the preservation of cultural heritage was equally important. Enslaved Africans brought with them their languages, religions, and traditions, which became vital aspects of their identity and resistance.

Through song, dance, storytelling, and oral traditions, enslaved communities maintained a sense of unity and resilience in the face of oppression. These cultural practices not only served as a reminder of their humanity but also became powerful tools for organizing and mobilizing communities.

The legacy of resistance against slavery would not be complete without acknowledging the vital role played by the abolitionist movements. These movements emerged throughout history and were composed of individuals who passionately campaigned for the abolition of slavery. They were a diverse group, consisting of both black and white activists, religious leaders, intellectuals, and former slaves who dedicated their lives to the abolitionist cause.

The 19th century saw the rise of prominent abolitionist figures such as Frederick Douglass, Sojourner Truth[1], and Harriet Beecher Stowe. Their eloquent speeches, powerful writings, and personal testimonials captivated audiences and evoked a profound sense of empathy and moral outrage. It was through their tireless efforts that the abolitionist movement gained momentum and eventually led to significant legislative changes, such as the Emancipation Proclamation in the United States.

The ongoing struggles for equality continue to this day, as the fight for freedom and justice takes new forms in our modern society. While slavery may have been legally abolished, its vestiges still linger, and systemic racism continues to permeate various aspects of our lives. It is our collective responsibility to perpetually strive for equality and to dismantle the oppressive structures that persist.

Commemorating the achievements of those who fought for freedom is of paramount importance in this ongoing struggle. Their stories serve as powerful reminders of the indomitable human spirit and the capacity for change. By honoring these individuals and sharing their stories, we ensure that their legacy lives on and that the ideals they fought for remain relevant.

Various forms of commemoration have emerged over the years, ranging from statues and memorials to annual celebrations and educational curricula. These efforts aim to not only educate people about the history of slavery but also to inspire future generations to continue the fight for equality.

The legacy of resistance against slavery and the abolitionist movements is a testament to the triumph of the human spirit. From the acts of rebellion and escape to the preservation of cultural heritage, the enslaved

Africans demonstrated immense courage and resilience. The abolitionist movement comprised of individuals from all levels of society and races played a vital role in shaping public opinion and advocating for legislative changes.

Slavery Systems

Ancient Slavery in Greece and Rome

We are aware that enslavement was a horrific but common thread in our history. In the forgoing chapters we will speak about the types of systems that were prevalent in their day.

Greece

Greece, slavery was ubiquitous, entrenched in the social fabric of the city-states. Slaves, also known as douloi[li], were considered property, devoid of any substantial rights or agency. They were derived from a variety of sources, including war captives, those born into slavery, and debtors who found themselves in servitude as a means of settling their obligations.

The roles of slaves in ancient Greece were multifaceted, ranging from domestic chores to more specialized tasks. Some slaves were employed as agricultural labourers, toiling away in the fields under the scorching sun. Others found themselves in the households of the wealthy, tasked with managing household affairs, caring for the children, and attending to the needs of their masters and mistresses.

Slaves were also used as skilled artisans, contributing their talents to the flourishing art and cultural production that characterized ancient Greece. Their work as potters, painters, and craftsmen was instrumental in shaping the aesthetic landscape of the time. However, it is important to note that while these slaves may have possessed certain skills, they were still the property of their masters, and their labour was extracted without just compensation or freedoms.

Conditions for slaves in ancient Greece were undoubtedly harsh, with the well-being of the enslaved often taking a backseat to the whims and desires of their masters. While some slaves may have experienced relatively lenient treatment, many others fell victim to the cruelty and dehumanization that defined the institution of slavery.

Physical punishment was commonplace, with some slaves enduring beatings or even torture for perceived transgressions. Slaves were subject to sexual exploitation and abuse, with their bodies treated as objects to be used and discarded at will. The dignity and humanity of the enslaved were systematically eroded, resulting in a deeply degrading and demoralizing existence.

The implications of slavery on ancient Greek society were far-reaching, deeply intertwined with its very fabric. Slaves were not only essential to the functioning of households but also played a significant role in the economy. Their labour, often unpaid and coerced, provided the backbone for agricultural production and contributed to the accumulation of wealth by the slaveholding elite.

The system of slavery also had profound effects on social hierarchies and power dynamics. The existence of a vast population of slaves allowed the citizen class, who were free men, to maintain their elevated status and the privileges that came with it. This created a stark divide between the enslaved and the free, establishing a rigid social structure that perpetuated inequality and exploitation.

Rome

In Rome, the institution of slavery was equally prevalent, if not even more deeply entrenched. Slaves, or servus, were an integral part of Roman society, forming a sizable portion of the population. Slavery in Rome was largely based on conquest, with war captives brought in as property to be bought, sold, and used as a form of labour.

Roles for slaves in Rome were vast and varied. Like their Greek counterparts, they were often consigned to domestic duties, taking care of household tasks, and tending to the needs of their masters. Slaves were also employed in agriculture, mining, and construction, contributing to the economic prosperity of the empire.

However, the treatment of slaves in Rome was not uniform. While some enslaved individuals may have fared relatively better, enjoying a certain level of autonomy and upward mobility, many others suffered under the weight of their bondage. The Roman legal system offered little protection to the enslaved, with their lives and well-being at the mercy of their owners.

The harsh reality of slavery in Rome was epitomized by the most deplorable institution within the system: the gladiatorial games. Slaves, along with criminals and prisoners of war, were forced to fight to the death for the entertainment of the masses. The lives of these gladiators were inherently disposable, with their bodies and skills commodified for the enjoyment of others.

The implications of slavery in Rome mirrored those of Greece, with the institution deeply intertwined with societal structures and the economy. Slavery perpetuated an unequal distribution of wealth and power, with a select few slaveholders amassing vast fortunes while the enslaved languished in servitude.

The presence of slavery also had profound consequences for social cohesion within the empire. As the number of slaves increased, so too did fears of rebellion and social unrest. The Roman elite employed various methods to control their enslaved populations, such as harsh discipline, surveillance, and punishment. These measures not only served to maintain the status quo but also fueled deep-seated resentments and tensions between masters and their slaves.

These great empires, with all their advancements and achievements, were also complicit in the dehumanization and degradation of countless individuals. The implications of slavery on the lives of the enslaved were manifested in physical and psychological trauma, as well as the erosion of basic human dignity. The roles of slaves within society and the economy were essential, their labour contributing to the accumulation of wealth and the maintenance of social order. Yet, this contribution came at a great cost, perpetuating an unequal distribution of power and denying the enslaved their inherent rights as human beings.

Slavery in the Islamic World

Slavery, as an institution in the Islamic World, predates the arrival of Muslims. However, it was during this time that the rules and regulations surrounding enslavement were solidified and incorporated into the legal framework of the faith. Islamic teachings provided guidelines on the humane treatment of slaves, encouraging their emancipation, and advocating for their fair treatment in society. Despite these principles, it is important to acknowledge the dichotomy between the idealized Islamic teachings and the actual practice of slavery within the Islamic World.

The Arab slave trade[lii], which spanned over a millennium, served as one of the primary conduits for the acquisition and dispersal of slaves within the Islamic World. African slaves were captured and sold by various African groups involved in the trade, with the profits primarily benefiting Arab and Muslim merchants. This lucrative trade operated along pre-existing Saharan trans-Saharan routes and expanded to include coastal regions. The demand for African slaves was propelled by the labour-intensive industries such as agriculture, mining, and domestic work.

Within the Islamic societies, slaves held diverse roles and were integrated into various spheres of life. They served as domestic workers, agricultural labourers, soldiers, concubines, administrators, and even scholars. The very fabric of Islamic societies was interwoven with the presence of slaves, shaping its cultural, economic, and social dynamics. In households, slaves were responsible for performing menial tasks, managing households, and raising children. A skilled slave could hold advantageous positions within society, with some achieving significant prominence and influence.

Despite the ideals espoused by Islamic teachings, the reality of the treatment slaves faced varied greatly. While some were treated with kindness and respect, others endured harsh conditions and maltreatment. The extent to which the humane treatment of slaves was practiced was influenced by a myriad of factors, including the geographic location, the specific interpretations of Islamic teachings, and the personal beliefs of slaveholders themselves.

The cultural impact of slavery in the Islamic World cannot be ignored, as it left its mark on the societies in which it thrived. African slaves brought with them their distinct cultural traditions, languages, and belief systems, influencing the artistic, culinary, and linguistic landscapes of their new homes. In some cases, they assimilated into the local culture and adopted Islamic practices, creating a unique blend of African and Islamic traditions. However, it is essential to acknowledge that this adaptation was – as we have seen with African slaves - often accompanied by a loss of cultural identity and the erosion of ancestral ties.

Economically, the institution of slavery played an integral role in the prosperity of Islamic societies. The labour provided by African slaves propelled agricultural and industrial sectors, allowing for economic growth and the accumulation of wealth. Slaves were considered valuable assets, with their acquisition and sale being a profitable business venture for merchants and traders. The economic reliance on slavery became deeply entrenched, resulting in a socio-economic structure that elevated the status of slaveholders and entrenched the marginalization of slaves.

In terms of social dynamics, the presence of slaves within Islamic societies created a distinct hierarchy, with slaveholders occupying the apex of the social ladder. Slaves, on the other hand, were relegated to the lowest rungs of society and subjected to varying degrees of discrimination and disenfranchisement. The complexity of social relations within these societies depended on numerous factors, including the status and wealth of the slaveholder, the origins of the slave, and the specific roles they performed.

The Arab slave trade and the roles played by slaves within Islamic societies were not static, but rather dynamic and evolving over time. Slavery was not simply a phenomenon experienced by Africans but spanned across various racial, ethnic, and religious groups.

Slavery in the Caribbean and Latin America

Plantation Economies:

In both the Caribbean and Latin America, the plantation system formed the backbone of the colonial economies. These sprawling plantations, primarily cultivating cash crops such as sugar, tobacco, and coffee, relied heavily on slave labour to maintain profitability. The abundance of fertile land and favorable climatic conditions in these regions made them perfect for large-scale agricultural operations.

In the Caribbean, particularly in countries like Jamaica, Barbados, Trinidad, and Haiti, the plantation system reached unprecedented levels of wealth and productivity. The demand for cane sugar fueled the expansion of the slave trade, as plantation owners sought to acquire more bodies to toil in the fields.

In Latin America, countries such as Brazil, Colombia, and Cuba also witnessed the rise of plantation economies. While sugar remained a significant crop, other products like tobacco, coffee, and cocoa gained prominence. The vastness of the landscapes allowed for the establishment of large plantations, and as a result, the demand for enslaved labour skyrocketed.

Treatment of Slaves:

The treatment of slaves in the Caribbean and Latin America bore striking similarities to American slavery, but there were also notable differences. Slaves in all regions endured backbreaking labour, physical and psychological abuse, and the constant denial of basic human rights. However, the specific nuances of the slave systems shaped the experiences of enslaved individuals.

In the Caribbean, the sheer intensity and brutality of the sugar plantations meant that slaves had some of the shortest life expectancies. The grueling labour involved in sugarcane cultivation required slaves to work long hours under the scorching sun, resulting in rampant exhaustion and illness. The high mortality rates necessitated a constant influx of new slaves to sustain the plantation workforce.

In Latin America, the treatment of slaves was often influenced by the racial hierarchy that existed in these societies. Slavery in this region was deeply entrenched in a complex system of racial categorizations, with a greater emphasis on colour distinctions. Slaves with a lighter skin tone, known as "mulattos," were often granted slightly better treatment and more opportunities for advancement compared to those with darker skin.

Cultural and Social Implications:

The institution of slavery in the Caribbean and Latin America left an indelible mark on the cultural and social fabric of these regions. Enslaved Africans brought with them their rich cultural traditions, which defiantly survived the oppressive conditions of plantation life. The fusion of African, European, Indigenous and later East Indian influences gave rise to vibrant cultural expressions, such as music, dance, and religious practices.

In the Caribbean, the African diaspora strongly influenced the development of music genres like Reggae[liii], Calypso[liv], Chutney[lv] and even Zouk[lvi]. These musical forms became powerful tools for resistance and empowerment, enabling enslaved individuals to maintain a sense of identity and unity. Similarly, folkloric dance traditions, like the Afro-Cuban Rumba and Haitian Vodou ceremonies[lvii], became vital outlets for cultural expression and spiritual connection.

In Latin America, the legacy of slavery is evident in various cultural manifestations. The influence of African customs can be seen in genres like samba and bossa nova in Brazil, cumbia in Colombia, and Afro-Cuban jazz in Cuba. Furthermore, religious syncretism, which combines elements of African spirituality with Catholicism, has given rise to unique belief systems such as Santeria in Cuba and Candomble in Brazil.

Socially, slavery profoundly impacted the racial dynamics of the Caribbean and Latin America. The legacy of colonialism and slavery created deeply entrenched racial inequalities that persist to this day. Skin colour and ancestry continue to play a significant role in determining social status and access to opportunities.

Yet, despite the horrors of slavery, the resilience and resistance of enslaved peoples in the Caribbean and Latin America are a testament to the strength of the human spirit. The struggles and triumphs of those who endured the brutality of the plantation system have shaped the cultural landscapes of these regions, enriching them with a diversity that is both a source of pride and a reminder of a painful past.

Slavery in Asia

There were various forms of slavery that pervaded Asia throughout history. Serfdom, for instance, was a prevalent system in many parts of Asia. Serfs, unlike chattel slaves, were tied to the land they worked on. They were not completely owned by their masters but were bound to their masters' estates, obligated to provide them with labour and tribute. In a sense, serfdom created a symbiotic relationship, where the serfs depended on the land for survival, while the masters relied on the labour of the serfs to maintain their wealth and power.

A significant part of enslavement in Asia was comprised of debt bondage. This system, which persists in some regions, is a stark reminder of the interplay between poverty and exploitation. Debt bondage arises when individuals, burdened by overwhelming debts, are forced to surrender their freedom to work off what they owe. They become trapped in a cycle of perpetual servitude, their labour exploited by creditors who hold the power to extend or increase their debts indefinitely.

Indentured labour was yet another form of slavery that plagued Asia for centuries. This system involved recruiting labourers from one region to work in another, often under coercive or deceitful circumstances. Indentured labourers, referred to as "coolies," were bound to labour contracts that ranged from five to ten years or even longer. They endured harsh conditions, meager wages, and relentless exploitation, all in the hope of escaping poverty and finding a better life for themselves and their families.

Cultural, economic, and social factors played a significant role in shaping these oppressive systems. Culture, with its deep-rooted traditions and societal norms, often provided a fertile ground for the acceptance and perpetuation of slavery. In many Asian cultures, the caste system or similar hierarchies enabled the justification of enslaving certain individuals deemed of lower social standing. The notion of superiority based on birth or occupation further entrenched these oppressive practices, making it challenging for individuals to break free from the chains that bound them.

Behind the veil, economic forces also played a pivotal role in perpetuating the Asian slave trade. Asia's rich resources, culinary delights, and exotic commodities made it a lucrative target for the European powers during the age of colonization. With an insatiable demand for labour to extract and cultivate these coveted resources, the European powers exploited and manipulated the existing systems of slavery to meet their economic aspirations. Deep in the bustling markets of Asia, human lives became commodities, bought, and sold for the purpose of fueling the insatiable hunger for profits.

Moreover, the social fabric of Asian societies, often marked by complex hierarchies and power dynamics, supported the continuance of slavery. The ruling elite, perpetuating their dominance, used slavery as a tool to amass wealth and maintain control over their subjects. At the same time, the oppressed found themselves not only grappling with their captors but also with their fellow slaves, as the system often pitted them against each other in a desperate scramble for survival.

Slavery in Asia was not a monolithic phenomenon, but multifaceted weave of the interplay of cultural, economic, and social factors. It left its own mark on the conscience of this vast continent and its people. It was a stain that could never be eradicated, a reminder of humanity's capacity to inflict suffering upon its own kind.

We cannot help but feel sorrow for the millions who had suffered under the yoke of bondage, rage at the systems that had perpetuated their suffering, and a sense of duty to bear witness to their stories.

Slavery Systems – Amerindian and African

The Amerindian slave trade predates the transatlantic African slave trade by centuries. Following the arrival of Christopher Columbus in the Americas, indigenous peoples were forced into enslavement by European colonizers. This brutal system involved the exploitation of Amerindian labour for economic gain and the subjugation of entire communities. Amerindians wilted under the weight of demand for output that their European masters placed on them. Their numbers dwindled because of disease, overwork, and starvation.

Comparatively, the African slave trade was a massive undertaking that spanned several centuries and forever transformed the face of the world. Millions of Africans were forcibly taken from their homes and forcefully transported across the Atlantic Ocean to work on plantations in the Americas. The transatlantic slave trade was characterized by its scale, with European powers utilizing Africans as a means of labour to drive their economies. The legacy of this institution is still felt to this day, as the African diaspora continues to grapple with the lasting effects of commodifying human beings.

Studying the comparison between these two systems uncovers a myriad of lessons. Firstly, it is evident that the enslavement of one group of people by another is a testament to the darkest corners of humanity's potential for cruelty. It is a stark reminder that power and greed can lead to the systematic dehumanization and subjugation of an entire race or ethnic group. By examining the historical context, we gain a greater understanding of the roots of racism and the institutionalized systems that continue to perpetuate inequality. Lessons learned from the enslavement of Amerindians were incorporated into the African slavery model.

The impact of these slavery systems on contemporary societies is undeniable. The forced migration of Africans to the Americas led to the formation of African diasporic communities. These communities, infused with rich cultural heritage, have played an integral role in shaping the social fabric and cultural identity of nations across the Americas. From art to music to literature, the contributions of the African diaspora cannot be overstated. However, the legacy of slavery also burdened these communities with a complex history of trauma, discrimination, and systemic barriers that continue to be felt today. Understanding the historical context of these systems is essential for dismantling these barriers and creating a more just and inclusive society.

The comparative study of slavery systems shed light on the resilience and strength of those who survived these atrocities. The resistance movements that arose during this time, such as the Maroon communities in the Americas, are a testament to the unyielding spirit of enslaved individuals. These communities, formed by escaped slaves, fought back against their oppressors, establishing independent settlements and waging guerrilla warfare against colonial powers. Their stories serve as a reminder that even in the darkest moments of human history, there is hope and longing for freedom.

The world is still grappling with the legacies of slavery and the perpetuation of systemic racism, understanding the historical context of these atrocities is of utmost importance. It allows us to better understand, challenge and dismantle the systems of oppression that have endured. Understanding its historical context, we gain a deeper understanding of the roots of racism, the impact on contemporary societies, and the importance of dismantling these oppressive systems.

Historical Perspectives

Eurocentric Vs. Afrocentric Perspectives

Throughout history, the interpretations and narratives surrounding the slave trade and American slavery have been shaped by various perspectives influenced by cultural and historical contexts. The Eurocentric and Afrocentric perspectives hold differing views on these topics, each providing unique insights into the implications and consequences.

Eurocentric perspectives on the slave trade and American slavery tend to emphasize economic and political factors, often downplaying the profound human suffering endured by African slaves. This perspective centers on the European expansion into the Americas, particularly through the establishment of colonies for the extraction of resources and the exploitation of labour. From an economic standpoint, Eurocentric scholars argue that the transatlantic slave trade was essential for the development of Europe and the Americas. They highlight the economic prosperity brought to European nations, as well as the financial benefits enjoyed by American plantation owners, all of which contributed to the growth of capitalist systems.

Eurocentric interpretations downplay or even justify the inhuman treatment of slaves by arguing that slavery was a societal norm at the time. They tend to present the narrative of slavery as an institution that was accepted and perpetuated by both Africans and Europeans. This perspective often fails to acknowledge the resistance and agency of African peoples, reducing them to passive victims of the trade rather than active participants in resistance movements and struggles for liberation.

In contrast, Afrocentric perspectives place greater emphasis on the experiences and struggles of African peoples, seeking to reclaim their history and give voice to those who were silenced. Afrocentric scholars aim to challenge Eurocentric distortions and present a more comprehensive understanding of the slave trade and American slavery. They argue that African societies were not passive participants but were often coerced or manipulated into participating in the trade through violence, deception, and exploitative trade practices imposed by European powers.

The Afrocentric perspective seeks to highlight the resilience, resistance, and survival of enslaved African peoples. It emphasizes the cultural and intellectual contributions of African civilizations, arguing that the slave trade was an act of cultural genocide that attempted to erase the rich heritage and diversity of African cultures. Afrocentric scholars often delve into African oral traditions and literature to unearth narratives of resistance, emphasizing the role of abolitionists, maroons, and other freedom fighters in challenging the institution of slavery.

Moreover, the Afrocentric perspective addresses the psychological and social consequences of slavery on African diasporic communities. It explores the enduring impact of slavery and engages in discussions around racism, discrimination, and systemic oppression, recognizing how these legacies continue to shape the experiences of African descendants today. By centering African voices and experiences, Afrocentric scholars aim to challenge the dominant, Eurocentric narratives that have historically marginalized their history and minimized their contributions to human civilization.

The implications of these perspectives go beyond mere academic discourse. The Eurocentric perspective perpetuates stereotypes and reinforces a narrative that positions Africans as inferior and passive subjects, thereby perpetuating racial prejudices and inequalities. This perspective often ignores the structural and systemic injustices that continue to impact African diasporic communities, leading to erasure and the perpetuation of harmful stereotypes.

In contrast, the Afrocentric perspective fosters a sense of empowerment and pride among African diasporic communities, encouraging cultural preservation, resilience, and the pursuit of social justice. By challenging dominant narratives, Afrocentric scholars encourage a more inclusive understanding of history that recognizes the agency and contributions of African peoples throughout the centuries.

It is essential to engage in critical discourse and explore these differing perspectives, allowing for a more nuanced and holistic understanding of the slave trade and American slavery. This means acknowledging the economic motivations and impacts, as well as the human suffering that took place. By intertwining the Eurocentric and Afrocentric viewpoints, we can strive towards a more comprehensive historical narrative that acknowledges the complexities of this painful and transformative period in human history.

To bridge the gap, we must all try to take an unbiased view. This however requires that we continue to walk this delicate tightrope while we examine the various narratives, interpretations, and implications surrounding the slave trade and American slavery.

Revisionist Interpretations

One of the most significant challenges to traditional narratives is the revaluation of historical sources. As would be expected, many of the primary sources that historians have relied on for information about the slave trade were written by those who directly benefited from it. Slave traders, plantation owners, and other powerful figures had a personal stake in ensuring that their actions were justified and that their profits remained secure. As a result, these sources often downplayed the brutality and dehumanization of enslaved people and portrayed a narrative that justified and perpetuated their subjugation.

Revisionist historians have sought to show alternative sources and perspectives that offer a more nuanced understanding of the slave trade. Instead of relying solely on the records of those in power, they have turned to the accounts of enslaved people themselves. By examining slave narratives, oral histories, and other firsthand testimonies, some historians offer a counter-narrative that gives voice to the experiences and perspectives that have long been suppressed.

In addition to revaluating the sources, revisionist interpretations also challenge the traditional narratives by questioning the motivations and actions of those involved in the slave trade. Previously, it was often assumed that the enslavement of Africans arose simply from a desire for economic gain. While this was undoubtedly a significant factor, revisionist historians have pointed out that the motivations behind the trade were far more complex and layered.

They argue that the slavery system was not only driven by economic greed but also by deeply embedded racism and a desire for dominance and control. The dehumanization and commodification of Africans allowed Europeans and Americans to justify their actions and maintain their position of power. By interrogating these motivations, revisionist interpretations offer a more comprehensive understanding of the forces at play during this time.

Reference Poems
Hidden In Plain Sight – Book 3
- 1ne Race
- Tired
- The Reality of our Lives
- I don't want to World

The impact of these revisionist interpretations on our understanding of this history cannot be overstated. By challenging traditional narratives, they force us to confront and acknowledge the full extent of the horrors inflicted upon enslaved people. They demand that we grapple with the profound injustices that were committed and refuse to turn away from the uncomfortable truths that lie at the heart of this history.

Furthermore, these reinterpretations compel us to examine the ways in which the legacies of slavery continue to shape our world today. Slavery was not simply an event that happened in the past and then ended; its consequences and repercussions are still felt and witnessed today. By reframing our understanding of the slave trade and American slavery, revisionist interpretations highlight the ongoing struggles for equality and justice that are rooted in this history.

Gender and Slavery

We cannot lose sight of the negative impact enslavement had on enslaved women. Bound by the iron shackles of their masters, their bodies were commodified, their autonomy stripped away. They were subjected to physical and sexual violence, used as mere breeding machines. Furthermore, they were forced into laborious tasks that further eroded their spirit. Yet, despite the immense weight of oppression, these women demonstrated an indomitable spirit that resisted and persisted against all odds.

Reference Poems
The Lamentation of the Enslaved – Book 1
- A Changed Young Girl – Part I
- A Changed Young Girl – Part II
- Hidden Love Part I
- Hidden Love Part II
- A love letter from Preston to Feewar
- Feewar's Final Promise

Enslaved women played multifaceted roles within their enslaved communities. While some toiled in the fields alongside men, enduring the backbreaking labour, others found themselves confined to the interiors of households, serving as domestic labourers. These women bore the responsibility of maintaining the daily operations of their masters' households, cooking, cleaning, and caring for children. Simultaneously, they were often the primary caregivers for their own children, creating a delicate balance between their own family responsibilities and the demands imposed upon them by their masters.

The contributions of feminist scholarship have been instrumental in showing the history and experiences of enslaved women. Through their rigorous research and analysis, feminist scholars have challenged traditional historiography that often neglected the voices and experiences of women. By examining historical records, personal narratives, and oral histories passed down through generations, these scholars have pieced together a narrative that uncovers the resilience, agency, and resistance of enslaved women.

Research has unveiled the agency demonstrated by enslaved women in their quest for freedom. While some women used their acts of resistance to challenge their oppressors directly, such as sabotage or running away, others found more subtle means of defiance. These women employed various strategies to undermine the system of slavery – from deception and manipulation to the preservation of cultural practices that upheld their dignity and humanity.

In their quest for freedom, enslaved women forged alliances with other marginalized groups, including Indigenous peoples and free people of colour. By pooling their resources and sharing knowledge, these women created networks and support systems that were essential in their struggle for freedom. They formed bonds of solidarity and nurtured a collective spirit that became the undercurrent for social and political change.

Scholars have also explored the challenges faced by enslaved women, particularly in relation to gender-based violence. The atrocities inflicted upon them were often exacerbated by their gender, leaving them vulnerable to sexual exploitation and abuse. The systematic rape of enslaved women not only served as a means of asserting dominance and control but also perpetuated the cycle of enslavement through the birth of mixed-race children.

The forced separation of enslaved women from their families further compounded the trauma they endured, leaving them isolated and bereft of the support systems that provided solace in the face of adversity.

Memory and Commemoration

Museums play a pivotal role in shaping our understanding of the slave trade and American slavery. These institutions serve as repositories of historical artifacts, documents, and narratives that provide visitors with a tangible connection to the past. The exhibits in these museums not only educate the public about the realities of slavery but also aim to evoke empathy and promote dialogue on the ongoing repercussions of this dark period. From displays of slave ships to personal belongings of enslaved individuals, museums offer a glimpse into the lives of those who endured unimaginable hardships.

One museum that stands out in its dedication to preserving the memory of the slave trade and American slavery is the National Museum of African American History and Culture in Washington, D.C. This institution takes visitors on an immersive journey through the experiences of enslaved Africans, their fight for freedom, and their contributions to American society. It reminds us that history cannot be forgotten or swept under the rug; it must be faced head-on for us to fully grasp its consequences.

Memorials, on the other hand, provide physical spaces for remembrance and reflection. They serve as solemn reminders of the atrocities committed during the transatlantic slave trade.

Collective memory plays a crucial role in shaping our understanding of history. It is through the stories passed down from generation to generation that we preserve the narrative of slavery and its lasting impact. The African diaspora, for instance, has held onto traditions, songs, and folklore that not only commemorate the horrors of slavery but also celebrate the resilience and strength of those who survived.

Additionally, literature and art have served as powerful mediums for remembering and commemorating the slave trade and American slavery. Countless novels, poems, and artworks have emerged over the years, offering a creative outlet for artists to express their perspectives on this painful history. Their work not only prompts us to reflect on the past but also challenges us to question the present and envision a more just future.

The power of oral history cannot be underestimated. The descendants of those who were enslaved have kept their stories alive through family narratives, oral traditions, and community gatherings. These personal accounts provide invaluable insights into the lived experiences of enslaved Africans, their resilience, and their fight for freedom. And as time passes and the generations change, it becomes essential for us to document and preserve these oral histories to ensure that memory and commemoration continue to shape our understanding of this history.

Memorialization and commemoration play a vital role in understanding of the slave trade and American slavery. Museums, memorials, collective memory, literature, art, and oral history all contribute to a deeper appreciation of the past and its ongoing implications.

Teaching and Learning About Slavery

Education on the topic of slavery goes beyond simply memorizing dates and events; it is about understanding the deep-rooted societal issues that still resonate today. It is about acknowledging the legacy of slavery and how it has shaped our world in terms of racial inequalities, discrimination, and systemic oppression. Teaching and learning about the slave trade and American slavery should serve to confront the uncomfortable truths of our past, while also addressing the present social implications and striving towards a more just future.

Yet, navigating the challenges of teaching about slavery can be daunting. One challenge lies in the emotional toll it may take on both educators and students. The stories of enslaved individuals are not just historical accounts; they are narratives of trauma, resilience, and triumph over adversity. To teach this history effectively, educators must approach it with sensitivity and empathy, ensuring that the experiences of those who were enslaved are respected, honored, and accurately portrayed. This requires creating safe spaces for students to engage with this difficult subject matter and providing appropriate support for those who may be triggered by the content.

Another challenge is overcoming the pervasive myths and miseducation surrounding slavery. Many textbooks and historical narratives have perpetuated distorted views of slavery, deliberately ignoring or down-playing the true brutality and dehumanization experienced by enslaved Africans and African Americans. Consequently, education on slavery must involve unpacking these myths, deconstructing stereotypes, and presenting a more comprehensive and accurate understanding of the institution.

Curriculum development plays a crucial role in shaping how slavery is taught and understood. It is essential to include diverse perspectives in the curriculum, embracing the stories and voices of those who have been historically marginalized. This includes amplifying the experiences and narratives of enslaved people, as well as providing insights from indigenous populations who were also victims of enslavement by European colonizers. By incorporating diverse perspectives, students can gain a more nuanced understanding of the slave trade and slavery, moving towards a more inclusive and comprehensive education.

It is imperative to highlight both the resistance and agency of enslaved individuals in the curriculum. The narrative of slavery often emphasizes the powerlessness and victimhood of those who were enslaved, but this only perpetuates a one-dimensional portrayal of their experiences. By displaying acts of rebellion, the creation of community, and the preservation of culture, students can appreciate the resilience and strength demonstrated by enslaved individuals in the face of unimaginable adversity.

Inclusivity and diversity are not only important in the content of the curriculum but also in the way it is delivered. Educators must undergo training and professional development to ensure they are equipped to teach this sensitive subject effectively. Engaging with scholars, community leaders, and activists who have dedicated their lives to studying and understanding slavery can provide valuable perspectives and insights.

Experiential learning can be a powerful tool when teaching about slavery. Visiting historical sites, museums, and engaging in dialogue with survivors, or descendants of survivors, can provide a deeper understanding of the lived realities of enslaved individuals. These experiences foster empathy and personal connection, allowing students to comprehend the long-lasting impacts of slavery on individuals, families, communities, and societies.

Education is not an end in itself but a means to cultivate critical thinking, empathy, and a commitment to justice. It is through education that we can ensure the past is not forgotten and the ongoing fight for equality and liberation is carried forward.

Lessons From History

Addressing Systemic Racism

Dismantling systemic racism in various spheres of society, means acknowledging and confronting the historical roots of this injustice. The slave trade, which involved the forced migration and enslavement of millions of African people, was a foundation upon which the Americas was built. Africans were captured from their homes, torn away from their families, and subjected to brutal conditions as they were transported across the Atlantic to be sold as slaves on plantations. This dehumanizing practice forged a system that perpetuated racial inequality and oppression.

The history of American slavery teaches us that systemic racism is not solely an individual problem; it is deeply embedded within the structures and institutions of our society. Slavery was not just a personal act of cruelty but a legal and economic institution that spanned generations. Laws were enacted to legitimize the ownership of human beings, reinforcing the notion that one race was superior to another. These laws supported and perpetuated a system that denied African Americans even the most basic human rights.

The legacy of slavery did not end with the Emancipation Proclamation or the end of the Civil War.

It evolved into new forms of discrimination and oppression. The Black Codes and Jim Crow laws were implemented, segregating black and white communities, and further cementing racial divisions. African Americans were systematically denied access to educational opportunities, job opportunities, and political power. Generations of African Americans were deprived of the same opportunities for upward mobility that their white counterparts enjoyed.

Reference Poems
Freedom Bells are Ringing – Book 2
- The Black Codes
- Slavery by another name
- The Great Debate
- The White Man's League

The effects of slavery and its subsequent discriminatory policies are still visible in modern society. They have led to the creation of racial disparities in education, wealth, housing, and healthcare, among other areas. African Americans continue to face higher rates of poverty, lower rates of educational attainment, and limited access to quality healthcare, all of which are direct consequences of the systemic racism that has persisted since the days of slavery.

To address and dismantle systemic racism, we must first start with education. It is crucial to teach the history of slavery and its lasting impact on our society in a comprehensive and honest manner. This includes not only the stories of African American resilience and resistance but also the role that white people played in perpetuating slavery and benefiting from its legacy. By understanding our shared history, we can begin to empathize with those who have been marginalized and work towards building a more just society.

In addition to education, we must also work to reform institutions and policies that perpetuate systemic racism. This requires a commitment to dismantling discriminatory practices and creating more inclusive systems. The criminal justice system, for example, disproportionately targets and incarcerates people of colour. By advocating for criminal justice reform, we can address the systemic racism that underlies this issue.

Economic inequality is another area where systemic racism is deeply entrenched. African Americans face barriers to accessing employment opportunities and achieving economic mobility. By promoting equitable hiring practices, investing in minority-owned businesses, and expanding access to affordable housing, we can begin to address the economic disparities that have their roots in slavery and its aftermath.

Political representation is also crucial in dismantling systemic racism. African Americans have historically been underrepresented in positions of power and decision-making. By encouraging and supporting the political participation of people of colour, we can ensure that their voices are heard, and their interests are represented in policymaking.

It is important to recognize that addressing systemic racism requires ongoing and sustained efforts, not just temporary fixes. It requires a commitment to challenging our own biases, learning from the past, and actively working towards a future that is truly equal and just for all. We must all continue to challenge ourselves to recognize the connections between history and the present. It is only then that we can take meaningful steps towards dismantling systemic racism and building a more inclusive society.

Social Justice Movements

Looking back on the historical timeline of social justice movements, one cannot help but be awed by the resilience and determination of those who fought for justice in the face of adversity. From the abolitionist movement in the 19th century to the civil rights movement in the 20th century, each struggle has helped to make strides towards equality.

The abolitionist movement, which sought to end the slave trade, holds particular significance in understanding the legacy of social justice movements. It was a battle fought on multiple fronts, encompassing legal battles, political activism, and the relentless efforts of individuals who sought to expose the brutal horrors of slavery. The strength of the abolitionist movement lay in its ability to galvanize people from various backgrounds, uniting them through a shared belief in the intrinsic worth and dignity of every human being.

Fast forward to the civil rights movement, which emerged in the mid-20th century with the goal of eradicating racial segregation and discrimination. The movement employed nonviolent resistance tactics to challenge the oppressive Jim Crow laws and demand equal rights for African Americans. It was through collective action, such as the Montgomery Bus Boycott and the March on Washington, that the civil rights movement brought about tangible change and paved the way for the dismantling of segregationist policies.

What can we learn from these past struggles? One significant lesson is the power of unity and collective action. Social justice movements thrive when individuals come together, recognizing their shared humanity, and fighting for a more just society. The abolitionists, for example, united people from different social classes, including religious leaders, politicians, and everyday citizens, highlighting the strength that emerges when diverse voices join forces.

Another lesson lies in the importance of perseverance and resilience. Social justice movements are often met with fierce opposition, ingrained prejudice, and systemic barriers. Yet, the abolitionists and civil rights activists did not succumb to despair; they persisted in the face of adversity. Their determination serves as a reminder that progress is not always linear or swift, but rather a continuous struggle requiring unwavering commitment.

These historical movements highlight the significance of raising awareness and shining a light on societal injustices. The abolitionists utilized literature, speeches, and personal accounts to expose the horrors of slavery, effectively engaging the public's conscience and inspiring empathy. Similarly, the civil rights movement leveraged media coverage and powerful speeches to amplify their message and garner widespread support. Today, with the advent of social media and instant global communication, activists have an unprecedented ability to share their narratives and mobilize support for their cause.

In examining the connections between past and present social justice movements, it becomes clear that the fight for equality is far from over. While progress has been made in many areas, systemic injustices and inequalities persist, necessitating ongoing collective action. The contemporary movements for equality, such as the Black Lives Matter movement and the fight for LGBTQ+ rights, stand on the shoulders of historical giants, drawing inspiration from their tactics, resilience, and unwavering determination.

Moreover, the intersectionality of today's social justice movements highlights the interconnected nature of oppression and discrimination. Activists understand that the fight for justice cannot be limited to a singular cause; it must encompass a multitude of issues, recognizing the overlapping experiences of marginalized communities. Solidarity amongst different movements strengthens the collective voice and amplifies the demands for equality, challenging the structural and systemic barriers that perpetuate injustice.

The connections between historical social justice movements and contemporary movements for equality are undeniable. Through studying the past, we gain insight into the strategies, challenges, and triumphs of those who fought for justice before us. The lessons we learn from these struggles provide a roadmap for future activism, emphasizing the importance of collective action, perseverance, raising awareness, and recognizing the interconnectedness of various forms of oppression.

Healing and Reconciliation

The slave trade, particularly the transatlantic slave trade that dominated from the 16th to the 19th centuries, stands as one of the greatest atrocities in human history. Millions of African men, women, and children were torn from their homes, forcibly transported across the Atlantic, and subjected to dehumanizing conditions on plantations in the Americas. The physical and psychological trauma endured by enslaved Africans was profound and has left an indelible mark on the global landscape. This history has been perpetuated by systems of racism, discrimination, and unequal power dynamics, which continue to shape societies to this day.

To embark upon a journey of healing and reconciliation, it is crucial to acknowledge the pain and suffering inflicted upon African people by the slave trade and its subsequent manifestations. This act of recognition provides a foundation upon which the process of healing can begin. It requires society to acknowledge and confront the atrocities committed, not only on individual and community levels but also on systemic and institutional scales.

However, the challenges to healing historical wounds are manifold. The first obstacle lies in the acknowledgement itself. Many people, particularly those in positions of privilege, are resistant to facing the uncomfortable truths of history and acknowledging their own complicity in perpetuating systems of oppression. This resistance can manifest through denial, distortion, or minimization of the impact of slavery. Overcoming this resistance requires a collective effort of education and enlightenment, as well as a willingness to confront uncomfortable truths.

Another challenge is the intergenerational transmission of trauma. The trauma experienced by enslaved Africans has been passed down through generations, creating a legacy of pain and suffering. Decades of systemic racism and discrimination have reinforced this trauma, resulting in ongoing disparities in areas such as education, healthcare, and economic opportunity. To promote healing, it is crucial to address the intergenerational effects of trauma and provide resources and support for healing at an individual, family, and community level.

Moreover, the notion of reconciliation raises complex questions. How can reconciliation be achieved when the hierarchical power structures that were foundational to the slave trade continue to exist? How can true reconciliation be achieved in a society that has not fully reckoned with its past, nor made reparations for the crimes committed against African people? These are questions that challenge the very fabric of society and demand transformative change.

Reference Poems

Hidden In Plain Sight – Book 3
- My Brothers White
- My Brothers Black
- Duality

Fostering dialogue and creating spaces for healing is crucial. Dialogue allows for the exchange of stories, experiences, and perspectives, providing an opportunity for empathy, understanding, and solidarity. Healing circles, community forums, and intergenerational dialogues can be powerful tools in promoting healing and reconciliation. These spaces must be safe, inclusive, and facilitated by qualified professionals to ensure productive and respectful conversations.

To embark upon a journey of healing and reconciliation in the context of the slave trade and American slavery is not an easy task. It requires deep introspection, a willingness to confront uncomfortable truths, and a commitment to dismantling existing power structures. The challenges are vast, but so is the potential for transformation. By acknowledging the pain of the past, addressing intergenerational trauma, seeking truth, pursuing reparations, and fostering dialogue, society can move closer towards healing historical wounds and promoting true reconciliation.

Promoting Equality and Inclusion

Promoting equality and inclusion, as we've seen, begins by recognizing that injustices and inequalities have plagued humanity throughout history. The transatlantic slave trade serves as a grim reminder of the depths to which human greed and prejudice can sink. Millions of Africans were forcibly uprooted from their homeland, torn apart from their families, and subjected to unimaginable horrors as they were sold into a life of bondage. The legacy of this brutal trade is still felt today in the systemic racism and discrimination that persists in different forms across various societies.

It is essential for us to acknowledge this history and its consequences to foster empathy and understanding. By recognizing the atrocities committed in the past, we can work towards addressing the deep-rooted disparities that continue to affect marginalized communities. Through education and open dialogue, we can create a society that not only acknowledges the existence of these inequalities, but actively works to dismantle them.

Lessons learned from history can guide us in our quest for a more equitable and inclusive world. One such lesson is the power of collective action. Throughout history, marginalized groups have had to fight for their rights and demand equal treatment. From the abolitionist movement that fought to end slavery to the Civil Rights Movement in the United States, these struggles have shown us that change is possible when individuals come together and challenge the status quo.

Strategies for creating a more equitable and inclusive world must address both systemic and individual prejudices. Systemic changes can be achieved through policy reforms and legislation that promote equality and protect the rights of marginalized communities. Affirmative action programs, for example, aim to level the playing field by providing opportunities for historically disadvantaged groups.

However, legislative measures alone are not enough. True inclusion requires a shift in societal attitudes and perceptions. This can be achieved through education and raising awareness about the experiences and contributions of marginalized communities. By highlighting the rich diversity of our society and promoting understanding and acceptance, we can create a world where everyone feels valued and included.

It is also crucial to actively address implicit biases and prejudices that may exist within individuals.

Unconscious biases can manifest in subtle ways, influencing our decisions and interactions without our awareness. Recognizing and challenging these biases is an ongoing process that requires self-reflection and a willingness to unlearn harmful stereotypes.

We can also promote equality and inclusion by fostering representation and diversity in positions of power and influence. When decision-making bodies reflect the society they serve, the needs and concerns of all members are more likely to be considered. This can be achieved by actively seeking out diverse voices and perspectives and creating platforms for underrepresented groups to tell their stories and contribute to the shaping of policies and institutions.

Promoting equality and inclusion also involves creating safe spaces where marginalized communities can share their experiences and be supported. These spaces provide an opportunity for healing, empowerment, and collective action. By providing platforms for marginalized voices to be heard and amplified, we can break down barriers and challenge the dominant narratives that perpetuate inequality.

History has taught us the consequences of prejudice and discrimination, and it is our responsibility to learn from these lessons. By addressing systemic inequalities, challenging individual biases, and fostering representation and diversity, we can work towards a world where everyone's voices are heard, valued, and included.

Brian Sankarsingh

A Final Thought

Education plays a crucial role in shaping our understanding of the past and its impact on the present. First, we must be unafraid to delve into history to gain a deeper understanding of the complex dynamics that have shaped society. It is through education that we uncover the stories of those who have been marginalized and silenced, shedding light on their struggles and triumphs. The history of the slave trade, for instance, unveils the horrific atrocities inflicted upon millions of people, providing a stark reminder of the depths of human cruelty. By engaging with this history, we can challenge the narratives of oppression and domination that persist today.

Remembrance, too, is an essential component of historical awareness. Through commemorative events, memorials, and rituals, we honor the lives and legacies of those who have suffered under the yoke of enslavement. It is through remembrance that we acknowledge the pain and injustice that have scarred our collective past, allowing us to confront uncomfortable truths and reckon with our own complicity. By preserving the memory of those who have been oppressed, we ensure that their stories are never forgotten and that the lessons of history are imprinted upon our collective consciousness.

Empathy, the most powerful force in fostering a compassionate and just society, is intricately linked to historical awareness. As we learn about the struggles and resilience of those who came before us, we develop a deeper understanding of the human experience. We recognize the common threads that connect us with people who lived in separate times and faced different challenges. Through empathy, we can step into the shoes of others, feel their pain, and recognize the significance of their fight for freedom and equality. It is through empathy that we dismantle the barriers of indifference and forge connections that transcend time and space, driving us towards a more inclusive and equitable society.

The Civil Rights Movement in the United States serves as testament to the power of historical awareness. Through acts of civil disobedience, marches, and speeches, activists like Martin Luther King Jr. and Rosa Parks brought the injustices faced by African Americans to the forefront of national consciousness. By invoking the historical legacy of slavery and segregation, they not only highlighted the systemic oppression faced by their community but also called upon individuals of all races to challenge and dismantle racial inequality. Their unwavering commitment to justice in the face of violence and adversity demonstrated the transformative power of historical awareness in driving social change.

There are countless stories of individuals who have exemplified the power of historical awareness in their pursuit of justice. These stories are available in poetry form in the accompanying books The Lamentation of the Enslaved, Freedom Bells are Ringing and Hidden in Plain Sight which form the series Enslaved, A Chronicle of Resistance. The books capture the beginning of African enslavement, Emancipation and Segregation and the book three focuses on systemic racism. It was my duty as a writer and poet to ensure that their voices were heard, their stories told. The power of historical awareness cannot be underestimated in shaping our present and future. Through education, remembrance, and empathy, we can challenge dominant narratives, honor the lives of those who have been oppressed, and foster a more compassionate and just society. Only through understanding and confronting our history can we hope to forge a future rooted in equity, empathy, and justice.

Through this series of books on the enslavement of Africans, I hoped to pay homage to the strength and resilience of those who had endured the unimaginable. Their cultural legacy lives on within the hearts and minds of their descendants, forever shaping the Americas into the diverse and vibrant society it has become.

Reference Poems
Hidden In Plain Sight – Book 3
- Colour Blindness

About the Author

SANKARSINGH is a Trinidadian-born Canadian immigrant who has published several books of poetry on a wide range of social and historical themes including racism, colonialism and enslavement. These topics are intimately intertwined with Sankarsingh's professional work with the Alliance for Healthier Communities. Sankarsingh artfully blends prose and poetry into his storytelling creating an eclectic mix with both genres. This unique approach is sure to provide something for everyone.

His debut book, A Sliver of a Chance, received several 5-star reviews from The Prairies Book Review, BookView Review, Red Headed Book Lover, OnlineBookClub and Readers Favourite.

Make sure to read,

Enslaved, Chronicle of Resistance Book I
The Lamentation of the Enslaved

And

Enslaved, Chronicle of Resistance Book II
Freedom Bells are Ringing

And

Enslaved, Chronicle of Resistance Book III
Hidden in Plain Sight

Index

[i] Black and White: Why capitalization matters - https://www.cjr.org/analysis/language_corner_1.php
[ii] Facts about the Slave Trade and Slavery - https://www.gilderlehrman.org/history-resources/teacher-resources/historical-context-facts-about-slave-trade-and-slavery
[iii] The Nri Kingdom (900AD-Present) - https://thinkafrica.net/nri-nigeria/
[iv] Partus Sequitur Ventrum Law Race and Reproduction in Colonial Slavery - https://blogs.law.columbia.edu/abolition1313/files/2020/08/Morgan-Partus-1.pdf
[v] Haiti Revolution of 1791 - https://en.wikipedia.org/wiki/Haitian_Revolution
[vi] Toussaint Louverture - https://www.britannica.com/biography/Toussaint-Louverture
[vii] Jean Jacques Dessalines - https://en.wikipedia.org/wiki/Jean-Jacques_Dessalines
[viii] Dutty Boukman - https://vocalafrica.com/epic-dutty-boukman-story-prayer/
[ix] The Jamaican Uprising aka the Baptist War - https://en.wikipedia.org/wiki/Baptist_War
[x] Samuel Sharpe - https://en.wikipedia.org/wiki/Samuel_Sharpe
[xi] Slavery Abolition Act 1833 - https://www.thecanadianencyclopedia.ca/en/article/slavery-abolition-act-1833
[xii] Maroon Community - https://www.britannica.com/topic/maroon-community
[xiii] Nat Turner - https://www.history.com/topics/black-history/nat-turner
[xiv] Denmark Vesey - https://www.britannica.com/biography/Denmark-Vesey
[xv] Frederick Douglass - https://www.biography.com/activists/frederick-douglass
[xvi] Harriet Tubman - https://www.britannica.com/biography/Harriet-Tubman
[xvii] Sojourner Truth - https://www.womenshistory.org/education-resources/biographies/sojourner-truth
[xviii] William Lloyd Garrison - https://www.britannica.com/biography/William-Lloyd-Garrison
[xix] Harriet Beecher Stowe - https://en.wikipedia.org/wiki/Harriet_Beecher_Stowe
[xx] John Brown - https://www.britannica.com/biography/John-Brown-

American-abolitionist
xxi Plessy v. Ferguson Summary - https://www.britannica.com/event/Plessy-v-Ferguson-1896
xxii Grandfather clause - https://www.britannica.com/topic/grandfather-clause
xxiii Brown v Board of Education - https://www.archives.gov/education/lessons/brown-v-board
xxiv Rosa Parks - https://www.britannica.com/biography/Rosa-Parks
xxv Montgomery Bus Boycott - https://www.history.com/topics/black-history/montgomery-bus-boycott
xxvi Martin Luther King Jr. - https://www.britannica.com/biography/Martin-Luther-King-Jr
xxvii March on Washington - https://www.britannica.com/event/March-on-Washington
xxviii Full text to the I Have a Dream speech by Dr. Martin Luther King Junior - https://static.pbslearningmedia.org/media/media_files/Full_text_I_Have_a_Dream_.pdf
xxix The Civil Rights Act 1964 - https://www.archives.gov/milestone-documents/civil-rights-act
xxx John Robert Lewis - https://en.wikipedia.org/wiki/John_Lewis
xxxi The Selma to Montgomery Marches 1965 - https://en.wikipedia.org/wiki/Selma_to_Montgomery_marches
xxxii Voting Rights Act (1965) - https://www.archives.gov/milestone-documents/voting-rights-act
xxxiii Medgar Evers - https://www.npr.org/2023/06/12/1180727818/medgar-evers-civil-rights-60-years
xxxiv The Murder of Chaney, Goodman and Schwerner - https://en.wikipedia.org/wiki/Murders_of_Chaney,_Goodman,_and_Schwerner
xxxv Loving v Virginia - https://supreme.justia.com/cases/federal/us/388/1/
xxxvi The Civil Rights Act 1964 - https://www.archives.gov/milestone-documents/civil-rights-act
xxxvii The Voting Rights Act 1965 - https://www.archives.gov/milestone-documents/voting-rights-act
xxxviii The Haitian Revolution - https://www.thoughtco.com/haitian-revolution-4690762
xxxix Olaudah Equiano - https://americanhistory.si.edu/on-the-water/learning-resources/life-sea/equiano
xl William Wilberforce (1759 - 1833) - https://www.bbc.co.uk/history/historic_figures/wilberforce_william.shtml

[xli] The Slave Trade Act 1807 - https://editions.covecollective.org/chronologies/historical-event-slave-trade-act-1807

[xlii] Harriet Beecher Stowe - https://www.biography.com/activists/harriet-beecher-stowe

[xliii] The British and Foreign Anti-Slavery Society, 1838–1956 - https://academic.oup.com/book/12262?login=false

[xliv] William Still - https://en.wikipedia.org/wiki/William_Still

[xlv] Levi Coffin - https://en.wikipedia.org/wiki/Levi_Coffin

[xlvi] Treaty of Madrid (13 January 1750) - https://en.wikipedia.org/wiki/Treaty_of_Madrid_(13_January_1750)

[xlvii] VIII. Final Text of the Dutch-American Treaty of Amity and Commerce: A Translation - https://founders.archives.gov/documents/Adams/06-13-02-0162-0011-0002

[xlviii] Congress of Vienna 1815 - https://www.britannica.com/facts/Congress-of-Vienna

[xlix] The British-Portuguese Anti–Slave Trade Treaty of 1817 - https://opil.ouplaw.com/page/618

[l] Sojourner Truth - https://en.wikipedia.org/wiki/Sojourner_Truth

[li] Doulos - https://en.wikipedia.org/wiki/Doulos

[lii] History of the slave trade in the Arab world - https://en.wikipedia.org/wiki/History_of_slavery_in_the_Muslim_world

[liii] A Brief History of Reggae - https://www.thepalmsjamaica.com/brief-history-reggae-music-first-jamaica-world/

[liv] A History of Calypso - https://www.ncctt.org/new/index.php/carnival-history/history-of-carnival/history-of-calypso.html

[lv] Chutney music - https://en.wikipedia.org/wiki/Chutney_music

[lvi] A History of Zouk Music - https://whatatune.com/what-is-zouk-music-a-brief-history/

[lvii] What is Haitian Vodou - https://theconversation.com/what-is-haitian-voodoo-119621

www.ingramcontent.com/pod-product-compliance
Lightning Source LLC
Chambersburg PA
CBHW020930090426
42736CB00010B/1091